# WEBER'S
# CHARCOAL GRILLING
## THE ART OF COOKING WITH LIVE FIRE™

### BY JAMIE PURVIANCE

#### PHOTOGRAPHY BY TIM TURNER

*Sunset*

| | |
|---:|:---|
| **Author:** | Jamie Purviance |
| **Managing Editor:** | Marsha Capen |
| **Photographer and Photo Art Direction:** | Tim Turner |
| **Food Stylist:** | Lynn Gagné |
| **Assistant Food Stylists:** | Nina Albazi, Liza Brown |
| **Photo Assistants:** | Takamasa Ota, Christy Clow, Patrick Kenney |
| **Indexer:** | Rebecca W. LaBrum |
| **Color Imaging:** | Vicki LaVigne |
| **In-House Pre-Press:** | Amy Dorsch, Sara Sweeney |
| **Contributors:** | Bruce Aidels, Amy Anderson, Dave Biondi, Tom Capen, Russell Cronkhite, Eric Dominijanni, John Gerald Gleeson, Andy Griffith, Don Grissom, Denis Kelly, Pete Marczyk, Mike McGrath, Jim Minion, Derek Muller, David Shalleck, Tripp Rion, Arthur Sampson, David Scully, Marie Simmons, Michael Stevens, Melanie Tapia, Thy Tran |
| **Charcoal Fanatic Photo Credits:** | Kathryn Whitney Lucey, page 50; courtesy of Mike McGrath, page 70; Dan Hemenway, page 86; Dan Cannon, page 92; Michael Stevens, page 104; courtesy of Amy Anderson and Melanie Tapia, page 118; Kathleen Biondi, page 122; Rose Apodaca, page 158; courtesy of John Gerald Gleeson, page 164; Otto Schmidt (photo on left) and Marsha Capen (younger Tom), page 188; courtesy of Dave Scully, page 194; Christopher K. Law, page 220. Used with permission. |
| **Recipe Testers:** | Elaine Johnson, Bob and Coleen Simmons, Amy Vogler |
| **Weber-Stephen Products Co.:** | Mike Kempster Sr., Executive Vice President |
| | Sherry L. Bale, Director, Public Relations |
| **rabble+rouser, inc.:** | Christina Schroeder, Chief Rouser |
| | Marsha Capen, Content Queen |
| | Michael Stevens, Creative Director |
| | Shum Prats, Art Director |
| **Design and Production:** | Shum Prats, Stacy Ebright |
| **Sunset Books:** | Richard A. Smeby, Vice President, General Manager |
| | Bob Doyle, Vice President, Editorial Director |
| | Linda Barker, Retail Sales Development Manager |
| | Brad Moses, Special Sales |

10 9 8 7 6 5 4 3 2

ISBN-10: 0-376-02047-4
ISBN-13: 978-0-376-02047-5
Library of Congress Control Number: 2006939796

For additional copies of *Weber's Charcoal Grilling: The art of cooking with live fire™*, visit our web site at www.sunsetbooks.com or call 1-800-526-5111

www.weber.com®
www.sunsetbooks.com

# ACKNOWLEDGEMENTS

Of all the names listed on the previous page, the one at the top may be the most conspicuous, but it doesn't fairly reflect the efforts that so many others have made for this book.

Mike Kempster and Susan Maruyama championed the idea of a cookbook devoted entirely to the art of cooking with a live fire. I appreciate their trust in me to write it and their full encouragement all along the creative process.

While working on the recipes, I relied on a wide-ranging, knowledgeable team of recipe developers and testers. I especially want to thank Bruce Aidels, Russell Cronkhite, Elaine Johnson, Denis Kelly, David Shalleck, Tripp Rion, Bob and Coleen Simmons, Marie Simmons, Thy Tran, and Amy Vogler.

I offer special thanks to the many charcoal fanatics I interviewed. They taught me so much about grilling, and each of the fourteen people featured in the following chapters was patient beyond belief as I called again and again for more and more insights.

Tim Turner, a virtuoso with a camera, turned our recipes into visual wonders. He and his colleagues, Lynn Gagné, Nina Albazi, Liza Brown—along with Takamasa Ota, Christy Clow, and Patrick Kenney— immersed themselves in the challenges and rewards of live fires.

I can't imagine a better place than Lobel's of New York (www.lobels.com) for getting the meat used in the photographs. I am amazed by their careful butchering and the quality of their customer service, both online and in their store.

At every stage of this book's development, from the initial brainstorming to the last moments of proofreading, one person gave more than anyone. My editor and friend Marsha Capen was enormously generous with her time and talents. How lucky I am to work with such a thoughtful, resourceful person.

I owe a special debt of gratitude to all of the creative, dedicated people at rabble+rouser. Designers Michael Stevens, Shum Prats, and Stacy Ebright created vitality and grace in the face of my random collection of ideas. Their leader, Christina Schroeder, brought great instincts and solutions to each dilemma.

Many thanks to Vicki LaVigne for making the most of the photos, and to Amy Dorsch and Sara Sweeney for all the gorgeous final touches.

It is always a pleasure to work with the gifted people at Sunset Books. Thank you, Rich Smeby, Bob Doyle, and Linda Barker, for supporting this book and steering it in the right direction.

At the times when I needed fresh perspectives and enthusiasm, I turned to Sherry Bale and Kim Durk. Thanks to each of them for always teaching me something new and inspiring me to dream big.

Finally, I want to thank my wife, Fran, and our children, Julia, James, and Peter. They support the work I love and they endure the whole process, even when dinner for five nights in a row is a slightly new version of the same grilled recipe. For this and much more, I am eternally grateful.

# TABLE OF CONTENTS

Wherever you find this symbol in the book,
look for special tips about charcoal grilling.

LIVE FIRE WISDOM · WEBER'S CHARCOAL ·

# JAMIE PURVIANCE

Photograph by Henry Diltz

As a ten-year-old boy I began my fascination with charcoal grilling at a summer camp in New Hampshire. One night the girls from the camp across the lake were invited to join my boy's camp for a barbecue. At that age, the thought of socializing with girls confused me with an unsettling mix of exhilaration and dread, so when my camp counselor asked me to help the caterer unload some things from his pick-up truck, I welcomed the distraction.

"Do you know anything about grilling?" the caterer asked.

"No," I said.

"Well, have a seat," he replied, as he turned over a milk crate for me. A charcoal fire was already roaring in his grill. He began talking technique to me while reddish-orange flames blazed brilliantly against the darkening sky. I tried to pay attention to him, but I was mesmerized by the animated sparks that drifted toward the tops of the trees and disappeared without a trace.

He went to work on the fire with a long iron tool, smashing some of his largest coals and then raking the broken embers into a long, even slope that grew hotter and hotter as it neared the cooking grate. There he jockeyed hamburgers from one spot to another just as they were on the verge of charring. All the while the coals sputtered and flared, but he remained strangely calm and instinctive. Out in the wilderness on a warm summer evening, with the sweet smells of hickory and oak filling the air, I could tell he was enjoying this just as much as I was, maybe more.

The hamburgers that night were exceedingly rich and gratifying. I remember juices running down my chin and the stunned silence you experience when food is so good that you would rather not speak about it. You just want to keep eating. Today, when I smell burning charcoal, it triggers memories of that night and many more occasions in my life when live fires burned with exciting possibilities: summer holidays, street fairs, class reunions, picnics in the park, tailgate parties, fiestas, and barbecues in my own backyard.

People often ask me about whether to grill with gas or charcoal. I tell them that gas has attractive features but charcoal opens up experiences all its own. In the charcoal world, we prefer timeless methods to push-button convenience. We prefer the fickleness of a live fire to the predictability of propane. We prefer rustic smoky flavors to clean-burning gas. In other words, we take great pleasure in the eternal truths listed on the following page.

*Jamie Purviance*

# THE 3 ETERNAL TRUTHS
## ABOUT CHARCOAL

**1** Something deep in our human DNA drives us toward the primordial satisfaction of cooking over crackling flames and glowing embers. Each time we light a live fire we reconnect with generations of ancestors all the way back to the beginning of civilization.

**2** Every charcoal fire is like a snowflake—one of a kind—and part of its attraction lies in the challenge of responding to its particular way of burning. Part of its reward lies in improvising our own grilling styles.

**3** Anyone with half a taste bud can tell the difference that the woodsy aromas of a charcoal fire can make. There is no question that the type of charcoal we burn can flavor our food as much as any seasoning or sauce.

# MASTERING THE FIRE

Hundreds of thousands of years ago, some prehistoric ancestor of ours probably finished cooking his roast beast dinner over a campfire and kicked some dirt on the smoldering embers to put them out. He probably came back a few days later and saw that his embers had shrunk into black lumps. When he discovered that he could relight those shrunken lumps, he changed the course of outdoor cooking forever.

Today we call those lumps charcoal. For cooking purposes, they have significant advantages over wood logs. They burn hotter. They burn with less smoke. And they burn more evenly, which is a big deal, whether you are a prehistoric ancestor or a modern backyard griller.

# Types of Fuel

## Lump Charcoal

Today, the process of making lump charcoal typically begins by stacking wood logs in underground pits and covering them with sheet metal and dirt. The logs are lit at one end of the pile, and the wood smolders for a few days, during which time the oxygen-starved fire burns off water, sap, and other volatile substances. What's left is almost pure carbon, also known as char or lump charcoal.

Grilling over a lump charcoal fire is a dynamic experience, full of exciting challenges and rewards. As the coals begin to burn, they spark and crackle. When they reach their hottest temperatures, they sometimes pop explosively because of gasses trapped in gnarly pockets of the wood. Lump charcoal gets broiling hot pretty quickly, usually in 10 or 15 minutes. Its intense heat can sear food in seconds, browning the surface and scenting it with beautifully clean wood smoke aromas.

In many cases the smokiness emanates from one kind of wood only, such as mesquite or oak. Quite often though, a bag of lump charcoal will hold a mix of hardwoods: oak, hickory, maple, and possibly some tropical woods from South America or Asia. In terms of aromas, the differences between the hardwoods are subtle but still important. They don't differ as much as apples and oranges, but they do differ as much as various kinds of apples.

Once a lump charcoal fire gets to its hottest point, it begins to lose heat rather quickly. In many cases the temperatures will fall from high heat to medium heat in less than 30 minutes, so, if you want to maintain a certain temperature range for cooking, the fire needs replenishing. Fortunately lump charcoal lights and heats so quickly that you can get a burst of heat within 5 or 10 minutes of adding unlit coals.

## Hardwood Briquettes

For the sake of convenience, some charcoal briquette companies go a little further in their production processes. They crush their charcoal with a binder, usually a natural starch, so the compacted little pillows will hold their shape. Briquettes with no other additives are usually labeled "natural" or "hardwood." They burn almost as hot as lump charcoal, but they also burn out almost as quickly. Their major benefit is their evenness of size and shape. With these briquettes, it is relatively easy to create a smooth bed of coals, whereas the irregular shapes and sizes of lump charcoal can leave "holes" in the fire.

## Kingsford® Briquettes

Then there is America's most widely used brand of charcoal, Kingsford® briquettes. Kingsford adds mineral char (a soft coal to raise and prolong the heat), mineral carbon (a hard coal, also for raising and prolonging the heat), and limestone (a sedimentary rock to provide a coating of white ash) to their mix of crushed charcoal and cornstarch. Recently the company launched a grooved design that creates more surface area on each briquette, meaning they light faster now, usually in about 15 minutes. These briquettes produce longer and more even heat than lump charcoal or hardwood briquettes, and they cast a subtle smokiness on almost anything cooked above or beside them.

Briquettes burn longer than lump charcoal, so they need replenishing less often. But lump charcoal provides greater heat and more woodsy aromas. Why not use both? Many charcoal fanatics start their fires with a bed of slow-burning briquettes and add lump charcoal as needed.

# Lighting Charcoal

The simplest, most thorough way to light any kind of charcoal is to use a chimney starter—an aluminum cylinder with a handle outside and a wire rack inside. Remove the top grate (the cooking grate) from your grill and set the chimney starter on the charcoal grate below. Fill the space under the wire rack with a few sheets of wadded-up newspaper or a few paraffin cubes. Fill the space above the rack with the charcoal of your choice (lump or briquettes). Light the newspaper or paraffin cubes through the holes on the side. Lump charcoal will be burning strong and turning to ash along its edges in about 15 minutes. That's when the coals are ready for arranging on the charcoal grate. Briquettes can take anywhere from 15 to 30 minutes to fully light. Look for a light coating of white ash all over the briquettes. That's when they are ready for pouring onto the charcoal grate.

Another good method begins with placing a few paraffin cubes in the middle of the charcoal grate. Build a pyramid of charcoal over the paraffin cubes and then light the cubes. When the coals in the middle are lit, use tongs to pile the unlit coals on top. When all the coals are fully lit, arrange them on the charcoal grate as you like.

## How Much Charcoal Should I Use?

The amount of charcoal you need depends mostly on the size of your grill and the amount of food you plan to cook. The simplest way of measuring amounts of charcoal is with a Weber® RapidFire® chimney starter. Think of it as a measuring cup for charcoal. Filled to the rim (with 90 to 100 briquettes), a chimney starter will give you enough charcoal to spread in a single, tightly packed layer across about two-thirds of the charcoal grate of a standard 22½-inch-diameter kettle grill. Usually that is enough charcoal to cook a meal for 4 to 6 people. If you plan to grill longer than 30 minutes, you will probably need to add more charcoal. Because of the irregular shapes and sizes of lump charcoal, it is more difficult to tightly pack a chimney starter, so after you have poured the chimney of burning lump charcoal onto the charcoal grate, add at least a few more fist-size lumps to be sure your fire is spread wide enough across the charcoal grate.

Not using enough charcoal is a crucial and common mistake. The charcoal must extend at least 4 inches beyond every piece of food on the cooking grate above. Otherwise the food will not cook evenly.

Paraffin cubes provide odorless, non-toxic fuel for lighting charcoal.

A Weber® RapidFire® chimney starter also works as a "measuring cup" for charcoal. Filled to the rim, it provides the right amount of coals for most of the fires you will need.

# The Two-Zone Fire

## Easy as 1-2-3

1. Fill a Weber® RapidFire® chimney starter to the rim and burn the coals until they are lightly covered with ash.

2. Spread the coals in a tightly packed, single layer across one-half to three-quarters of the charcoal grate.

3. Put the cooking grate in place, close the lid, and let the coals burn down to the desired heat. Leave all vents open.

### Combining Direct and Indirect Heat

The basic two-zone fire is an efficient charcoal arrangement for a wide array of foods. It combines both direct heat (where the food cooks directly above the coals) and indirect heat (where the food cooks above and to the side of the coals). It is important to have both kinds of heat available at once, particularly when you are cooking with a live fire. Direct heat is best for relatively small, tender pieces of food that cook quickly, such as hamburgers, steaks, chops, boneless chicken pieces, fish fillets, shellfish, and sliced vegetables. Direct heat sears the surfaces of those foods, developing flavors and texture, and it cooks relatively thin foods all the way to the center. Indirect heat is best for larger, tougher foods that require longer cooking times, such as roasts, whole chickens, and ribs. Indirect heat cooks the surfaces of food, too, but in a much more even way.

To judge high, medium, or low heat, use the "hand test" on page 15.

# Measuring Heat

### How Hot Is It?

Grilling with the right level (or levels) of heat is just as important as the way you arrange the coals. Charcoal grilling does not require anything like the precision of baking or candy-making but, then again, trying to grill everything over the same level of heat oversimplifies charcoal grilling and misses big opportunities for superior tastes and textures.

There are really two ways of knowing how hot a charcoal fire is. One is to use the thermometer in the lid of your grill, that is, if your grill has one. If you grill often with indirect heat (barbecued chicken, pork ribs, prime rib), I strongly recommend a grill with that feature. Otherwise you will be tempted to lift the lid too often, just to see how the coals are doing, and that causes troublesome peaks and valleys in your cooking temperatures.

### The Hand Test

The other way to know the heat is to extend your palm over the charcoal at a safe distance. Imagine a soda can is standing on the cooking grate, right over the coals. If your palm was resting on the top of the can, it would be 5 inches from the cooking grate. That's where you should measure the heat of charcoal. Always pull your hand away from the heat before it hurts, and be sure that nothing flammable, such as a sleeve, is dangling from your arm. If you need to pull your hand away after 2 to 4 seconds, the heat is high. If you need to pull your hand away after 5 to 7 seconds, the heat is medium. If you need to pull your hand away after 8 to 10 seconds, the heat is low.

| Heat | Temperature range | When you will need to pull your hand away |
|---|---|---|
| High | 450°F to 550°F | 2 to 4 seconds |
| Medium | 350°F to 450°F | 5 to 7 seconds |
| Low | 250°F to 350°F | 8 to 10 seconds |

# The Three-Zone Sloped Fire

M

### Multitasking Charcoal

The basic two-zone fire handles adaptations easily. For example, you may want a three-zone sloped fire for certain recipes, with high heat on one side of the grill, medium heat in the middle, and indirect heat on the other side. To do this, pile the coals two or three briquettes high on one side of the grill and create a slope toward the opposite side of the grill. As always, leave at least one-third of the charcoal grate empty for indirect heat on the opposite side. This sloped arrangement gives you the flexibility to grill a few different foods at once, each requiring a different level of heat, as in the case of the shrimp tacos here. The shrimp are searing over high heat, the vegetables are cooking over medium heat, and the package of tortillas is warming over low (indirect) heat.

> To judge high, medium, or low heat, use the "hand test" on page 15.

# The Three-Zone Split Fire

### Even Indirect Heat

You can also adapt the basic two-zone fire for a three-zone split fire, where the coals are separated into two equal piles on opposite sides of the charcoal grate. Here you have two zones for direct heat (high, medium, or low) and one zone between them for indirect heat. This arrangement works well for cooking a roast over indirect heat, such as a pork loin or beef tenderloin, because you have the same level of heat on either side of the roast, assuring you of even doneness.

Placing a disposable pan between the coals and filling it about halfway with water allows you to catch drippings and to extend the life of your grill by keeping it clean. Additionally, the water both absorbs and releases heat, so a filled pan means you will need to add charcoal less often to maintain the temperature of your grill. The charcoal baskets help to keep the coals clustered together so they burn longer.

To judge high, medium, or low heat, use the "hand test" on page 15.

### A Matter of Opinion

Part of a charcoal fire's attraction is that it allows you the flexibility to arrange the fire in any number of ways. It welcomes personal preferences and improvisation. I know many grillers who usually cover the entire charcoal grate with coals. Some grillers like to build the coals much closer to the cooking grate. Some prefer to make a ring of coals around the perimeter of the charcoal grate and leave the middle zone empty for indirect heat. Play with the possibilities and do whatever works for you.

Frankly, for indirect heat I generally prefer a basic two-zone fire over a three-zone split fire. I like having the coals arranged on one side of the food only, because that allows me to adjust the heat applied to the food simply by moving the food closer to or farther away from the coals. Also, I sometimes want a little more heat on one side of what I am cooking than the other. For example, by facing the legs of a whole chicken toward the fire, I cook that side, where the dark meat is, a little hotter. If I need to even out cooking, I just turn the food around.

# Tending the Fire

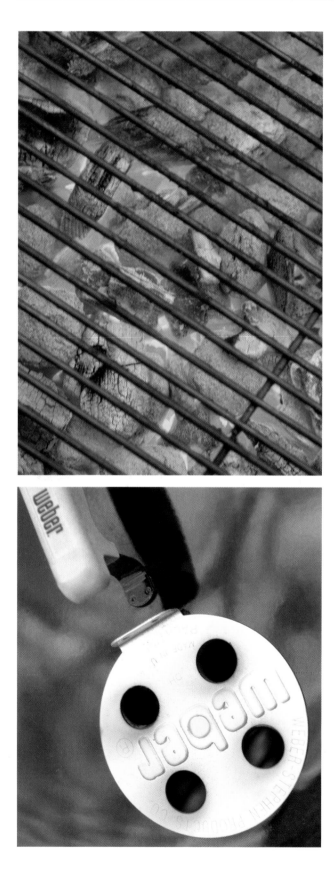

M

One of the more significant differences between gas and charcoal grilling is that with charcoal you are not only grilling food, you are also tending a fire. You are responsible for rearranging and replenishing the coals in whatever ways the food requires. While gas flames will burn patiently and wait until you are ready to cook, a charcoal fire has its own natural course. Without you, it will get hot and then burn out.

## Maintaining the Heat

In most cases you will simply want to maintain the heat of your fire. Left alone in normal circumstances, a lump charcoal fire will lose about 100°F over the course of 20 to 30 minutes. A typical briquette fire will lose about the same amount of heat over 30 to 40 minutes. To maintain the temperature in the same general range, you need to add new coals about every 30 minutes or so. How many? Well, that depends on several factors.

The first factor is, of course, what kind of charcoal you are adding. Lump charcoal lights faster and gets hotter than ordinary briquettes, so you can wait until just 5 to 10 minutes before you need its burst of heat. That is especially true of the smallest pieces, but remember that they will burn out quickly, so you will need to add them more often. Larger lumps take a little longer to get hot, but they also last longer.

If you want to minimize how often you need to replenish your fire, choose slow-burning briquettes. Remember that they take 15 minutes or more to reach their highest heat, so plan ahead. Or better yet, light the briquettes ahead of time in a chimney starter and add them when they are hot and covered in ash.

## Adjusting the Vents

Another major factor is air. The more air you allow into the grill, the hotter the fire will grow (to a point) and the more often you will need to replenish it. So to minimize replenishing, keep the lid closed as much as possible. The vents on the bottom of the grill should be left open whenever you are grilling, but to slow the rate of your fire's burn, close the top vent as much as halfway.

### Sweeping the Ashes

Allowing too much ash to accumulate on the bottom of the grill is a common mistake. This covers the vents, starves the coals of air, and lowers the heat quickly. Every 30 minutes or so, gently sweep the vents clear of ashes.

### Getting a Feel for It

Maintaining a charcoal fire is not as complicated as it might sound. Start by adding 10 to 12 briquettes (or an equivalent amount of lump charcoal) every 30 minutes or so. After you have done it a few times and felt the effects, you will develop a knack for it and you will fine-tune the timing for your particular charcoal of choice. Some people are frustrated by the lack of certainty about exactly how many coals to add at exactly what time. For charcoal fanatics, getting a feel for what each individual fire needs is a rewarding pursuit worth doing again and again.

# Tending the Fire

## Raising and Lowering the Heat

The most straightforward way to raise the heat of your fire is to add more fuel. As with maintaining the heat at a certain level, the amount you should add depends on the kind of charcoal, the size of the charcoal, and the amount of air feeding the fire. But roughly speaking, you will need ¼ to ½ of a Weber® RapidFire® chimney starter filled with briquettes (or an equivalent amount of lump charcoal) to raise your fire's temperature from low to medium or medium to high.

If you want to lower the heat in your grill, simply remove the lid and let the coals burn down. Use the hand test on page 15 to check the heat periodically. To speed up this process, spread the coals a little farther apart.

If your fire is burning with large lumps of charcoal, you can achieve a quick rise in temperature by breaking the large lumps apart. With more surface area exposed to the air, the coals will quickly burn much hotter.

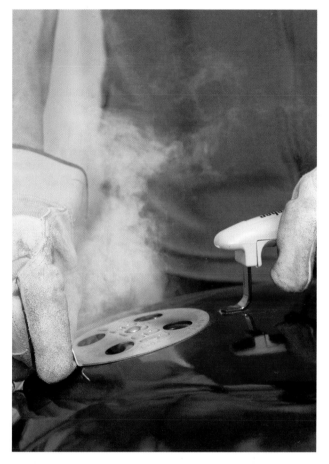

Your first response to flare-ups should be reducing the amount of air. If the lid is off, put the lid on and close the top vent about halfway.

## Dealing with Flare-Ups

Flare-ups occur when fat drips on the coals and ignites. A little bit of flaring is inconsequential. When the flames barely lick the surface of the food, you have no problem. Actually the flames will help to sear the surface of the food with excellent flavors. But when flames shoot through the cooking grate and threaten to burn the food, you need to respond.

One response is limiting the amount of air getting to the fire. If the lid is off, put it on and close the top vent about halfway. You will be surprised how many times this technique will put out flare-ups. You can check the status by looking through the partially open vent. If the flames are still threatening your food, open the lid and move the food over indirect heat. That's one reason why you should always have an area of indirect heat available. Usually after a matter of seconds, the fat in the fire burns off and the flare-ups are gone. Then you can return your food to direct heat.

If necessary, move the food over indirect heat until the flare-ups subside.

## Smoking on a Charcoal Grill

A kettle grill has excellent design features for smoking many kinds of food. The large bowl on the bottom allows you to build a small charcoal fire on one side and place a water pan on the opposite side. The water pan not only catches drippings from the food above, but more importantly, the water absorbs and releases heat along with a little bit of steam. Without the water pan, the charcoal fire would burn faster and you would need to replenish the coals more often.

A hinged cooking grate makes it easy to add more charcoal and wood. The type of charcoal and wood you add will make noticeable differences. For the long, slow cooking required for smoking, I recommend using briquettes. It is very difficult to maintain a small charcoal fire with lump charcoal alone. The temperatures tend to rise and fall too quickly, with unfortunate results in the food. With briquettes, you should have good success maintaining a low fire by adding 8 to 10 briquettes every 45 minutes or so. Having a thermometer on the lid is very helpful. For most smoked foods, you will want to keep the heat in the range of 250°F to 350°F. When you open the top vent fully, the heat will rise. As you close the top vent a little bit at a time, the heat will fall.

There is a tendency for many beginners to add wood to the fire as soon as the previous batch burns out—and to keep this up until the cooking is done. This quickly leads to overly smoked foods. Start with just a few handfuls of wood and taste the results. If you like your food a little smokier, add an extra handful next time.

## Chips or Chunks?

Your next choice is whether to add wood chips or wood chunks for smoke. Either will do nicely. The main difference is that chips burn faster than chunks. If you plan to add just a handful or two of chips for a light smoke over 20 minutes or so, then the burn rate is not a real issue. But if you want to smoke your food for an hour or more, it might be more convenient to use chunks. Depending on their size and the amount of air getting to the fire, they will burn that long, or even longer. If you soak chips or chunks in water for at least 30 minutes before adding them to the fire, you will prolong their burn significantly and they will smolder more than flame. Just be sure to drain the wood of water first so you don't extinguish the fire.

You could fill football stadiums with the wide-ranging opinions of which woods taste better with which foods. Ultimately, you should decide for yourself. But for the sake of keeping the debate alive, here are my general preferences. Like all preferences, they tend to vary based on whatever is working at the time. It takes only a taste of some new recipe with an unexpectedly great combination of wood smoke and meat to make me rethink my usual choices.

| Wood Pairings | |
| --- | --- |
| Beef and Lamb | oak and hickory |
| Pork | pecan, cherry, and apple |
| Chicken | apple and pecan |
| Fish | mesquite and alder |
| Vegetables | rosemary sprigs |

Always avoid soft, resinous woods like pine, cedar, and aspen. Never use wood that has been treated with chemicals.

M

# Smoking on a Water Smoker

If you find yourself captivated by the effects of wood smoke and you seek the meltingly tender results that only a very low fire can produce, you must have a water smoker. The Weber® Smokey Mountain Cooker™ smoker is an iconic piece of equipment in the barbecue world because it is very efficient at maintaining temperatures well below 300°F. Many top cooks and competitors have had their best successes with the simple technology of this smoker, which is affectionately know as the WSM.

1. To get started, fill the charcoal chamber with 1 chimney starter filled with charcoal briquettes.

The key is moderating the heat by opening and closing the vents on the bottom. The less air you allow into the fire, the lower the heat will go. The ideal temperature range is 225°F to 250°F. A good water smoker can keep temperatures in that range for more than 12 hours without any added charcoal.

4. Remove the lid, put the bottom cooking grate in place, and set the food on top.

M

2. Fill the chimney starter about halfway with more briquettes and light them. When the briquettes are ashed over, spread them evenly over the unlit briquettes.

3. Put the middle section in place and fill the water pan about three-quarters with warm water. Put the lid on and preheat the smoker for about 1 hour, with the top and bottom vents completely open.

5. Put the top cooking grate in place and set the food on top. Then put the lid on and make sure the top vent is open. The cooking temperatures will be the same at both the bottom and top cooking grates.

6. Open the side door and add wood chips/chunks for smoke.

# More Fun with Charcoal

## Cooking in the Coals

For a truly medieval experience, skip the cooking grate altogether and cook right in the coals (or right next to them). This primitive technique does amazingly good things for firm vegetables with sturdy skins. Take onions, for example. Though their skins burn over the course of an hour or so, their insides turn as tender and sweet as ripe fruit. Simply peel away the skins and enjoy luscious roasted onions scented with wood smoke. Other good choices for this technique are corn (still in their husks) and potatoes.

## Planking

Planking achieves some of the same culinary effects as smoking but with one special advantage. A smoked fillet of fish displayed on a plank makes a show-stopping presentation. Just be sure to set the plank on a heat-proof surface.

# Planking 101

1. SOAK THE PLANK IN WATER. Choose a container large enough for the plank and water, and weigh the plank down with something heavy so it doesn't float to the top. Soak the plank for at least 1 hour.

2. PREHEAT THE GRILL for medium heat. Meanwhile, prepare your food to the point that it is ready to cook. For example, remove it from its marinade or season it.

3. HEAT THE PLANK ON THE GRILL over direct medium heat. Take it out of the water, place it flat on the cooking grate, and immediately close the lid. In a few minutes, you will hear the plank crackle and you will see smoke beginning to escape from the grill.

4. PUT YOUR FOOD ON THE PLANK. Place it in the middle of the plank, close the lid, and let it cook until it's done. Keep an eye on the grill. If you see lots of smoke pouring out of the grill, use a water bottle to spray the flames and put them out. Moving the plank over indirect heat will also prevent flare-ups. The sooner you close the lid, the sooner the flare-ups will go out.

5. REMOVE THE FOOD AND THE PLANK from the grill together. Pick up the plank with sturdy tongs and lay it down on a heat-proof surface. Serve the food on the plank or on individual plates.

## More Fun with Charcoal

### Rotisserie Cooking

Food that slowly revolves above burning embers will baste itself with internal juices as it absorbs the flavors of the fire. For best results, split the burning charcoal into two equal piles on opposite sides of the charcoal grate and place a large, disposable drip pan between them. Fill the drip pan about halfway with warm water. Leave the lid off while the coals burn down to medium heat. Meanwhile, secure the food on the spit, making sure that it is centered as evenly as possible and that the counterweight is placed opposite the food's heaviest side. Put the rotisserie ring on the grill and plug in the motor. When ready to cook, set the spit in place, turn on the motor, and close the lid.

1. Each chicken should be trussed so that it holds a tight, even shape on the spit (see page 244).

2. Each prong of each fork should go deep inside the meat.

3. The chickens should be centered on the spit.

4. Chickens aren't your only option for the rotisserie. Also try turkey, duck, leg of lamb, and prime rib.

M

## Cooking with a Basket

A fish basket with one hinged side makes it very easy to cook and turn whole fish without the risk of the skins sticking to the cooking grate. It also allows you to move the fish closer to the coals or farther away from them, depending on how much heat you want at any given moment. In some cases, though, the skin has a tendency to stick to the basket itself, so line the basket with lemon slices or lettuce leaves.

A perforated basket is the solution to foods that are just too small or too many to turn individually. The perforations let charcoal aromas drift onto the food while juices and fat drip into the coals. For evenness of cooking, hold the edge of the basket with an insulated mitt and shake it, or use a spatula to turn the food over.

# RUBS, MARINADES, AND SAUCES

Now that you've learned how to harness the heat and flavors of a charcoal fire, let's consider the savory effects of rubs, marinades, and sauces. Rubs are usually mixtures of dried spices that not only add interesting tastes but also textures in the surface crusts of your food. Marinades can work in similar ways, though their wet flavors seep in a little deeper. Sauces are the final flourish. Sometimes it's delicious to layer their flavors on top of what a rub or marinade has already accomplished. Sometimes a sauce is so sublime, it's all you need to complement whatever you have grilled. The following pages hold some excellent possibilities for you.

# Rubs

## How Long?

If you leave a rub on for a long time, the seasonings intermix with the juices in the meat and produce more pronounced flavors, as well as a crust. This is good to a point, but a rub with a lot of salt and sugar will draw moisture out of the meat over time, making the meat tastier, yes, but also drier. So how long should you use a rub? Here are some guidelines.

| 1 to 15 minutes | Small foods, such as shellfish, cubed meat for kabobs, and vegetables |
|---|---|
| 15 to 30 minutes | Thin cuts of boneless meat, such as chicken breasts, fish fillets, pork tenderloin, chops, and steaks |
| 30 to 90 minutes | Thicker cuts of boneless or bone-in meat, such as leg of lamb, whole chickens, and beef roasts |
| 2 to 8 hours | Big or tough cuts of meat, such as racks of ribs, whole hams, pork shoulders, and turkeys |

## Classic Barbecue Spice Rub

4 teaspoons kosher salt
2 teaspoons pure chile powder
2 teaspoons light brown sugar
2 teaspoons granulated garlic
2 teaspoons paprika
1 teaspoon celery seed
1 teaspoon ground cumin
½ teaspoon freshly ground black pepper

**Makes about ¼ cup**

## Cajun Rub

2 teaspoons finely chopped fresh thyme
1½ teaspoons kosher salt
1 teaspoon granulated garlic
1 teaspoon granulated onion
1 teaspoon paprika
1 teaspoon light brown sugar
¾ teaspoon freshly ground black pepper
¼ teaspoon ground cayenne pepper

**Makes about 3 tablespoons**

## Asian Rub

2 tablespoons paprika
2 teaspoons kosher salt
2 teaspoons ground coriander
2 teaspoons Chinese five-spice powder
1 teaspoon ground ginger
½ teaspoon ground allspice
½ teaspoon ground cayenne pepper

**Makes about ¼ cup**

## Fennel Rub

3 teaspoons ground fennel seed
3 teaspoons kosher salt
3 teaspoons pure chile powder
1½ teaspoons celery seed
1½ teaspoons freshly ground black pepper

**Makes about ¼ cup**

# Marinades

## How Long?

The right times vary depending on the strength of the marinade and the food you are marinating. If your marinade includes intense ingredients such as soy sauce, liquor, or hot chiles and spices, don't overdo it. A fish fillet should still taste like fish, not a burning-hot, salt-soaked piece of protein. Also, if an acidic marinade is left too long on meat or fish, it can make the surface mushy or dry. Here are some general guidelines to get you going.

| | |
|---|---|
| **15 to 30 minutes** | Small foods, such as shellfish, fish fillets, cubed meat for kabobs, and tender vegetables |
| **1 to 3 hours** | Thin cuts of boneless meat, such as chicken breasts, pork tenderloin, chops, and steaks, as well as sturdy vegetables |
| **2 to 6 hours** | Thicker cuts of boneless or bone-in meat, such as leg of lamb, whole chickens, and beef roasts |
| **6 to 12 hours** | Big or tough cuts of meat, such as racks of ribs, whole hams, pork shoulders, and turkeys |

*Note: After a marinade has been in contact with raw fish or meat, either discard it or boil it for at least 30 seconds. The boiling will destroy any harmful bacteria that might have been left by the fish or meat. A boiled marinade often works well as a basting sauce.*

## Mojo Marinade

- ¼ cup fresh orange juice
- 3 tablespoons fresh lime juice
- 3 tablespoons extra virgin olive oil
- 2 tablespoons finely chopped fresh cilantro
- 1 tablespoon finely chopped jalapeño chile pepper, including seeds
- 1 tablespoon minced garlic
- ¾ teaspoon ground cumin
- ½ teaspoon kosher salt

**Makes about ¾ cup**

## Lemon-Sage Marinade

- 1 tablespoon finely grated lemon zest
- ¼ cup fresh lemon juice
- ¼ cup extra virgin olive oil
- 3 tablespoons finely chopped fresh sage
- 2 tablespoons minced shallot
- 2 tablespoons whole grain mustard
- 1 tablespoon finely chopped garlic
- 1 tablespoon freshly cracked black peppercorns

**Makes about 1 cup**

## Teriyaki Marinade

- 1 cup pineapple juice
- ½ cup low-sodium soy sauce
- ½ cup finely chopped yellow onion
- 1 tablespoon dark sesame oil
- 1 tablespoon grated fresh ginger
- 1 tablespoon minced garlic
- 1 tablespoon dark brown sugar
- 1 tablespoon fresh lemon juice

**Makes about 2 cups**

## Greek Marinade

- ¼ cup plus 2 tablespoons extra virgin olive oil
- 3 tablespoons red wine vinegar
- ½ teaspoon minced garlic
- ½ teaspoon kosher salt
- ½ teaspoon dried oregano
- ¼ teaspoon crushed red chile flakes

**Makes about ½ cup**

## Sauces

## White Barbecue Sauce

  1  large yellow onion
  2  medium garlic cloves
  4  tablespoons unsalted butter, cut into 4 pieces
  ½  cup dry white wine
  1  cup Miracle Whip® dressing
  ⅓  cup loosely packed, roughly chopped fresh tarragon
  ¼  cup apple cider vinegar (5% acidity)
  2  tablespoons fresh lemon juice
  1  tablespoon Dijon mustard
  1  tablespoon granulated sugar
  ½  teaspoon hot sauce, such as Texas Pete® or Tabasco®
  1  teaspoon sea salt
  1  teaspoon coarsely ground black pepper

Mince the onion and garlic until they are almost a paste. In a medium saucepan over medium heat, melt the butter. Add the onion and garlic, and cook until the mixture is opaque, 2 to 3 minutes, stirring occasionally. Add the white wine. Mix well and cook until half of the liquid has evaporated, 2 to 3 minutes, stirring occasionally. Remove the pan from the heat and let cool for about 5 minutes. Whisk in the remaining ingredients. The sauce should have the consistency of ranch dressing. Taste and adjust the seasonings, if desired. Cover and refrigerate until about 1 hour before serving. Store the sauce in the refrigerator for as long as 2 weeks.

**Makes about 2½ cups**

## Classic Red Barbecue Sauce

  ¾  cup apple juice
  ½  cup ketchup
  3  tablespoons cider vinegar
  2  teaspoons soy sauce
  1  teaspoon Worcestershire sauce
  1  teaspoon molasses
  ½  teaspoon pure chile powder
  ½  teaspoon granulated garlic
  ¼  teaspoon freshly ground black pepper

In a small saucepan mix the ingredients. Simmer for a few minutes over medium heat, and then remove the saucepan from the heat.

**Makes about 1½ cups**

## Black Olive Aioli

  ½  cup mayonnaise
  2  tablespoons black olive tapenade
  1  tablespoon fresh lemon juice
  1  teaspoon finely chopped fresh rosemary
  ¼  teaspoon freshly ground black pepper

In a small bowl whisk the ingredients until smooth. Cover and refrigerate until 30 minutes before serving.

**Makes about ¾ cup**

## Creamy Horseradish Sauce

  ¾  cup sour cream
  2  tablespoons prepared horseradish
  2  tablespoons finely chopped fresh Italian parsley
  2  teaspoons Dijon mustard
  2  teaspoons Worcestershire sauce
  ½  teaspoon kosher salt
  ¼  teaspoon freshly ground black pepper

In a medium bowl thoroughly mix the ingredients. Cover and refrigerate until 30 minutes before serving.

**Makes about 1 cup**

# Almond-Garlic Butter

  2  dozen whole almonds (about 3 tablespoons)
  3  large garlic cloves, peeled and left whole
  3  tablespoons unsalted butter, softened
  1  tablespoon finely chopped fresh dill
  ½  teaspoon kosher salt
  ¼  teaspoon freshly ground black pepper

In a medium skillet over medium heat, toast the almonds and garlic until darkened in spots all over, 4 to 6 minutes, turning occasionally. Remove the almonds and garlic from the skillet and let cool for a few minutes. With a large knife chop the almonds and garlic into tiny pieces (or pulse them in a food processor). In a small bowl combine the almond-garlic mixture with the remaining ingredients. Mash with the back of a fork until the ingredients are evenly distributed throughout the butter. Cover and refrigerate until about 1 hour before serving.

**Makes about ¼ cup**

# Tomatillo Salsa

  1  medium yellow onion, cut into ½-inch slices
     Extra virgin olive oil
 10  medium tomatillos, husked and rinsed,
     about ½ pound total
  1  small jalapeño chile pepper, stem removed
  ¼  cup lightly packed fresh cilantro leaves
     and tender stems
  1  medium garlic clove
  ½  teaspoon dark brown sugar
  ½  teaspoon kosher salt

Prepare a two-zone fire for high heat (see pages 14-15). Lightly brush the onion slices on both sides with oil. Brush the cooking grate clean. Grill the onion slices, tomatillos, and jalapeño over **direct high heat**, with the lid closed as much as possible, until lightly charred, 6 to 8 minutes, turning once or twice and swapping their positions as needed for even cooking. Be sure the tomatillos are completely soft as you remove them from the grill. Combine the onion slices, tomatillos, and jalapeño in a food processor along with the remaining ingredients. Process until fairly smooth. Taste and adjust the seasonings.

**Makes about 2 cups**

# Balinese Peanut Sauce

  ½  cup smooth peanut butter
  ½  cup stirred coconut milk
  2  tablespoons fresh lime juice
  2  teaspoons chile-garlic sauce, such as Sriracha
  2  teaspoons fish sauce

In a small saucepan combine the ingredients. Set the saucepan over very low heat and cook until the sauce is smooth, 3 to 5 minutes, whisking occasionally, but do not let the sauce simmer. If the sauce seems too thick, whisk in 1 to 2 tablespoons of water.

**Makes about 1¼ cup**

# Cool Green Chile Sauce

  3  long Anaheim chile peppers
  3  scallions, root ends discarded,
     all the rest roughly chopped
  ¼  cup lightly packed fresh cilantro leaves
     and tender stems
  1  small garlic clove
  ½  cup sour cream
  ½  cup mayonnaise
     Finely grated zest and juice of 1 lime
  ¼  teaspoon kosher salt

Prepare a two-zone fire for high heat (see pages 14-15). Grill the chile peppers over **direct high heat**, with the lid open, until they are blackened and blistered in spots all over, 3 to 5 minutes, turning occasionally. Remove the chiles from the grill. When cool enough to handle, remove and discard the stem ends. Using a sharp knife, scrape off and discard nearly all the blackened skins. Roughly chop the remaining parts of the chiles and drop them into a food processor or blender. Add the scallions, cilantro, and garlic. Process to make a coarse paste, scraping down the sides once or twice. Add the remaining ingredients and process for a minute or two to create a smooth sauce. If it seems too thick, add a little water. Adjust the seasonings. Cover and refrigerate until 30 minutes before serving.

**Makes about 1½ cups**

# APPETIZERS

# Grilled and Chilled Gazpacho

**Prep time: 20 minutes**
**Chilling time: at least 8 hours**
**Grilling time: 10 to 12 minutes**

    6  large plum tomatoes
    3  medium red bell peppers
    2  medium red onions
       Extra virgin olive oil
    1  teaspoon kosher salt
    ½  teaspoon freshly ground black pepper
    2  cups reduced-sodium tomato juice,
       plus as much as 2 cups more for thinning out the soup
    ¼  cup finely chopped fresh basil
    1  tablespoon sherry vinegar
    ¼  teaspoon Tabasco® sauce
    ½  English cucumber, peeled, cut in half
       lengthwise, and seeded
    ½  cup sour cream

**1.** Prepare a two-zone fire for medium heat (see pages 14-15).

**2.** Core each tomato and cut in half lengthwise. Cut the peppers into wide lengthwise strips, discarding the core and seeds. Cut the onions crosswise into ½-inch slices. Set aside and refrigerate 2 strips of bell pepper and 2 slices of onion to be finely chopped for garnish. Lightly coat the remaining tomatoes, peppers, and onions with oil. Season with the salt and pepper.

Choose peppers with flat sides that you can easily slice off the core. The flatter the sides, the more surface area will caramelize on the hot cooking grate.

**3.** Brush the cooking grate clean. Grill the tomatoes and peppers over ***direct medium heat***, with the lid closed as much as possible, until the skins are blistered and the vegetables are tender, 6 to 8 minutes, turning once or twice and swapping their positions as needed for even cooking. At the same time, grill the

Firm-fleshed plum tomatoes hold their shape well, even after the grill has blistered their skins.

onions over ***direct medium heat*** until lightly charred and crisp-tender, 10 to 12 minutes, turning once or twice and swapping their positions as needed for even cooking. Remove the vegetables from the grill and let cool. If necessary, remove and discard any burnt pieces of the vegetables.

**4.** In a blender, working in batches if necessary, purée the vegetables and any accumulated vegetable juices with the tomato juice. Chill for at least 8 hours, preferably overnight.

**5.** When the grilled vegetable purée is thoroughly chilled, check the texture. If it seems too thick, add more tomato juice. Then add the basil, vinegar, and Tabasco® sauce. If desired, season to taste with additional vinegar, Tabasco® sauce, salt, and pepper.

**6.** Finely dice the reserved onion and bell pepper along with the cucumber. Serve the gazpacho in individual bowls, cold or at room temperature, topped with sour cream and diced vegetables.

**Makes 4 to 6 servings**

# Bruschetta with Grill-Roasted Beets and Goat Cheese

**Prep time: 20 minutes**
**Grilling time: 1 to 1½ hours**

**Topping**

- 3 medium golden beets, about 6 ounces each
  Extra virgin olive oil
- 2 scallions, white and light green parts, thinly sliced
- 2 teaspoons white wine vinegar
- 1 teaspoon finely chopped fresh thyme
- ¼ teaspoon kosher salt
- ¼ teaspoon freshly ground black pepper

- 5 ounces fresh goat cheese

- 12 slices Italian bread, each about ⅓ inch thick
  Extra virgin olive oil
- 1 large garlic clove

**1.** Prepare a two-zone fire for medium heat (see pages 14-15).

**2.** Trim the stem ends of the beets and any long roots. Scrub the beets clean under cool water and lightly coat them with oil. Grill over ***indirect medium heat***, with the lid closed as much as possible, until tender when pierced with the tip of a knife, 1 to 1½ hours (depending on size), turning once and swapping their positions as needed for even cooking. To maintain the temperature, add 10 to 12

unlit charcoal briquettes (or an equivalent amount of lump charcoal) every 30 to 45 minutes.

**3.** When cool enough to handle, rub or peel the skins from the beets, cut them into ¼-inch dice, and place in a medium bowl. Add 1 tablespoon of oil along with the remaining topping ingredients. Mix well.

**4.** In a small bowl mix the cheese with 2 tablespoons of water.

**5.** Lightly brush or spray the bread slices on both sides with oil. Brush the cooking grate clean. Grill the bread slices over ***direct medium heat***, with the lid open, until toasted, 2 to 4 minutes, turning once and swapping their positions as needed for even cooking. Remove the slices from the grill and brush vigorously on one side with the garlic clove. Spread some of the goat cheese on each slice and top with the beet mixture. Serve at room temperature.

**Makes 4 to 6 servings**

The advantage of using golden beets, rather than red ones, is that they will not color the goat cheese.

# Ember-Roasted Onion and Garlic Dip with Crispy Pita

**Prep time: 15 minutes**
**Grilling time: 24 to 38 minutes**

**Dip**
  2  medium yellow onions (skin on),
      cut in half through the stem
  4  large garlic cloves (skin on)
      Extra virgin olive oil
  1  can (15½ ounces) garbanzo beans, rinsed
  ½  cup sour cream
  2  tablespoons fresh lemon juice
  2  tablespoons finely chopped fresh dill
  ¾  teaspoon ground cumin
  ¾  teaspoon Worcestershire sauce
  ½  teaspoon kosher salt
  ¼  teaspoon freshly ground black pepper
  ⅛  teaspoon ground cayenne pepper

  6  pita bread pockets

**1.** Prepare a two-zone fire for medium heat (see pages 14-15).

**2.** Lay the onion halves, cut sides down, on a 16-inch square of heavy-duty aluminum foil. Nestle the garlic cloves between the onions. Drizzle a couple tablespoons of oil over the onions and garlic. Fold up the sides of the foil and seal the packet. Place the packet right on top of the charcoal and cook, with the lid closed, until a knife inserted through the foil slides easily in and out of the onions, 20 to 30 minutes, carefully turning the packet with tongs once or twice. Carefully remove the packet with tongs and let cool to room temperature.

**3.** Lightly brush each pita on both sides with oil. Brush the cooking grate clean. Working in batches of 3 or 4 pitas at a time, grill them over ***direct medium heat***, with the lid open, until crisp and toasted, 2 to 4 minutes, turning frequently and swapping their positions as needed for even cooking.

**4.** Open the packet and remove and discard the skins and hard stem ends from the onions and garlic. Place the roasted onions and garlic in a food processor. Pulse until almost puréed. Add all the remaining dip ingredients and process until quite smooth. Adjust the seasonings, if desired. Cut each pita into wedges. Serve with the dip.

**Makes 4 to 6 servings**

# Chicken and Poblano Quesadillas with Guacamole

**Prep time: 15 minutes**
**Marinating time: 3 to 4 hours**
**Grilling time: 14 to 21 minutes**

**Paste**

|   |   |
|---|---|
| 2 | large garlic cloves |
| 1 | jalapeño chile pepper, stem removed |
| 1 | cup tightly packed fresh basil leaves |
| 3 | tablespoons extra virgin olive oil |
| 2 | tablespoons tequila |
| 1 | teaspoon kosher salt |
| ½ | teaspoon freshly ground black pepper |

    2  boneless, skinless chicken breast halves,
       about 8 ounces each

**Guacamole**

|   |   |
|---|---|
| 2 | Haas avocados, pitted and skins removed |
| 1 | tablespoon fresh lime juice |
| 2 | medium garlic cloves |
| ¼ | teaspoon kosher salt |
| 1 | tablespoon finely chopped fresh cilantro |
| ⅛ | teaspoon freshly ground black pepper |

    2  medium poblano chile peppers, stems removed
    4  flour tortillas (10 inches)
    2  cups grated Monterey Jack cheese

**1.** In a food processor mince the garlic and jalapeño. Add the remaining paste ingredients and process until smooth. Smear the paste on all sides of the chicken breasts. Cover and refrigerate for 3 to 4 hours.

**2.** In a medium bowl mash the avocados with the back of a fork and immediately mix in the lime juice. Roughly chop the garlic, then sprinkle the salt over the garlic and, using the side of a knife, crush the garlic with the salt until you create a smooth paste (see page 64). Add the garlic mixture, cilantro, and pepper to the bowl. Mix well.

Score the avocado flesh in a diamond pattern so that when you scoop it out, it is already in pieces.

**3.** Prepare a two-zone fire for medium heat (see pages 14-15).

**4.** Brush the cooking grate clean. Grill the chicken over ***direct medium heat***, with the lid closed as much as possible, until the juices run clear and the meat is opaque in the center, 10 to 15 minutes, turning once and swapping their positions as needed for even cooking. At the same time, grill the poblano chiles over ***direct medium heat*** until evenly charred on all sides, 7 to 9 minutes, turning as needed. Remove from the grill and allow to cool. Cut the chicken into thin slices. Peel away the charred skins from the chiles and roughly chop the flesh.

**5.** Lay the tortillas in a single layer on a work surface. Evenly divide the chicken, chiles, and cheese over half of each tortilla. Fold the empty half of each tortilla over the filling, creating a half circle, and press down firmly. Grill the quesadillas over ***direct medium heat***, with the lid closed as much as possible, until well marked and the cheese has melted, 4 to 6 minutes, turning once and swapping their positions as needed for even cooking. Allow the quesadillas to cool for a minute or two before cutting into wedges. Serve warm with the guacamole spooned on the top of each wedge.

**Makes 4 to 6 servings**

# Chile-Glazed Chicken Wings with Toasted Sesame Seeds

**Prep time: 15 minutes**
**Grilling time: 18 to 20 minutes**

16  chicken wings, 3 to 3½ pounds, wing tips removed
 2  tablespoons vegetable oil
 1  teaspoon kosher salt
 ¼  teaspoon freshly ground black pepper

**Glaze**
 3  tablespoons sweet chili sauce
 3  tablespoons soy sauce
 2  teaspoons chili-garlic sauce, such as Sriracha
 1  teaspoon dark sesame oil
 ½  teaspoon grated fresh ginger

 1  tablespoon sesame seeds

**1.** Prepare a two-zone fire for medium heat (see pages 14-15).

**2.** Put the wings in a large bowl and evenly coat them with the oil, salt, and pepper. Set aside at room temperature for 20 to 30 minutes before grilling.

**3.** In a small bowl whisk the glaze ingredients.

**4.** In a medium skillet over medium heat, toast the sesame seeds until golden brown, 3 to 5 minutes, stirring occasionally. Pour the seeds into a cool container to stop the cooking.

**5.** Brush the cooking grate clean. Grill the wings over *direct medium heat*, with the lid closed as much as possible, until golden brown, about 10 minutes, turning occasionally and swapping their positions as needed for even cooking. Then lightly brush the wings with the glaze on both sides and grill until the meat is no longer pink at the bone, 8 to 10 minutes, continuing to turn, glaze, and swap their positions for even cooking (you may not need all of the glaze). Remove the wings from the grill and sprinkle the sesame seeds over the top. Serve warm or at room temperature.

**Makes 4 servings**

# Yakitori

**Prep time: 25 minutes**
**Grilling time: 7 to 10 minutes**

- 10 boneless, skinless chicken thighs, about 2 pounds, cut into 1- to 1½-inch chunks
- 1 tablespoon vegetable oil
- 1½ teaspoons kosher salt
- ¼ teaspoon freshly ground black pepper

- 8 wooden skewers, soaked in water for at least 30 minutes

**Sauce**
- ½ cup low-sodium chicken stock
- 3 tablespoons soy sauce
- 3 tablespoons mirin (sweet rice wine)
- 2 tablespoons fresh lemon juice
- 1 tablespoon light brown sugar
- ¼ teaspoon freshly ground black pepper

**1.** Prepare a two-zone fire for high heat (see pages 14-15).

**2.** In a medium bowl combine the chicken chunks with the oil, salt, and pepper. Mix well. Thread the chicken chunks through their centers on the top half of the skewers. The chicken chunks should touch, but do not cram them together. Refrigerate until ready to grill or as long as 2 hours.

**3.** In a small saucepan mix the sauce ingredients. Bring to a boil over medium-high heat and cook until the liquid is reduced to ½ to ¾ cup, about 5 minutes, stirring once or twice. Remove the saucepan from the heat.

**4.** Brush the cooking grate clean. Place a double-layer strip of aluminum foil on the cooking grate over the empty section of the charcoal grate. Grill the skewers over ***direct high heat***, with the bare wooden section of the skewers placed over the foil. Close the lid and cook until the meat is lightly charred on the surface, 4 to 5 minutes, turning once and swapping their positions

The foil protects the bare wood of the skewers from burning.

as needed for even cooking. Open the lid and begin turning and basting the chicken with the sauce (you may not need all of it) until fully cooked, 3 to 5 minutes, swapping their positions as needed for even cooking. Remove from the grill and serve warm.

**Makes 4 to 6 servings**

# Vietnamese Beef Rolls with Sweet Chili Sauce

**Prep time: 20 minutes**
**Grilling time: 6 to 8 minutes**

**Sauce**
- 3 tablespoons granulated sugar
- 3 tablespoons fresh lime juice
- 1 tablespoon thinly sliced green onions
- 1 tablespoon fish sauce
- 2 teaspoons chili-garlic sauce, such as Sriracha

**Filling**
- 1 pound ground chuck (80% lean)
- ¼ cup finely chopped roasted peanuts
- ¼ cup thinly sliced scallions
- 1 tablespoon finely chopped fresh mint
- 1 teaspoon fish sauce
- ½ teaspoon kosher salt
- ¼ teaspoon freshly ground black pepper

- 18 small grape leaves in brine, each 4 to 5 inches in diameter, drained and then soaked in water for at least 15 minutes
- 12 wooden skewers, soaked in water for at least 30 minutes
  Vegetable or peanut oil

**1.** In a small bowl mix the sauce ingredients with 1 tablespoon of water until the sugar is dissolved.

**2.** In a large bowl gently combine the ground chuck with the rest of the filling ingredients.

**3.** Drain the grape leaves. Place a grape leaf, smooth side down, on your work surface. Cut off and discard any protruding stem. Shape a heaping tablespoon of the filling

Place a small log of seasoned beef near the base of each grape leaf. Fold the bottom of the leaf up. Fold the sides to the center. Then roll the leaf into a cylinder.

into a small log and place it near the stem end. Fold the stem end of the leaf over the filling. Fold in each side of the leaf, then roll the filling tightly toward the tip of the leaf. If necessary, cut off and discard any excess leaf at the tip. Repeat with the remaining beef filling and grape leaves.

**4.** Place 3 rolls side by side. Push a skewer through all the rolls about 1 inch from their ends. Repeat with another skewer parallel to the first one. Double-skewer the remaining rolls. Lightly brush the rolls with oil on both sides.

**5.** Prepare a two-zone fire for medium heat (see pages 14-15).

**6.** Brush the cooking grate clean. Grill the rolls over *direct medium heat*, with the lid closed as much as possible, until the filling is fully cooked and slightly firm, 6 to 8 minutes, turning and swapping their positions as needed for even cooking. Serve warm with the dipping sauce.

**Makes 6 servings**

# Thin-Crusted Pizzas with Smoked Sausage and Mozzarella

**Prep time: 30 to 40 minutes**
**Grilling time: 4 to 10 minutes for each pizza**

### Dough
- 1 envelope (2¼ teaspoons) active dry yeast
- 1 teaspoon granulated sugar
- 4 cups all-purpose flour, plus more for kneading the dough
- 3 tablespoons extra virgin olive oil, plus more for oiling the dough
- 1 tablespoon kosher salt

### Toppings
- 2-3 cups good-quality, thick tomato sauce
- 1 pound smoked, dried sausage, finely chopped or thinly sliced
- 2 cups grated mozzarella cheese
- 1 cup grated fontina cheese
  Extra virgin olive oil
- 3 tablespoons finely chopped fresh basil

Let the dough "rise" in a warm place until it doubles its size.

Punch the dough down and press out most of the air.

**1.** In a very large bowl combine the yeast and sugar with 1½ cups warm water (105°F to 115°F). Stir for a few seconds to dissolve the sugar and let stand until foamy, about 5 minutes. Add 4 cups of flour, 3 tablespoons of oil, and the salt. Mix and knead with your hands until all the flour comes off the sides of the bowl and the dough holds together in a coarsely textured ball. Allow the ball to sit in the bowl at room temperature for 15 minutes. Transfer the dough to a lightly floured work surface and knead for 10 to 15 minutes. To test

if the dough has been kneaded enough, tear off a small piece. Pull and tug the dough from all sides. If the center tears easily, the dough needs more kneading. If you can stretch a paper-thin, translucent membrane of dough in the center (see above), it has been kneaded enough. Shape all of the dough into a ball and place in a lightly oiled bowl. Turn the ball to cover the surface with oil. Cover the bowl with a kitchen towel and set aside in a warm place until the dough doubles in size, 1½ to 2½ hours.

**2.** Prepare a two-zone fire for medium heat (see pages 14-15).

**3.** Punch down the dough in the bowl. Transfer to a work surface and cut into 8 equal pieces. Lightly brush eight,

12-inch squares of parchment paper on one side with oil. Using your fingers, flatten each piece of dough on a sheet of parchment paper to create 8 round crusts. Each crust should be about ¼ inch thick and 6 to 8 inches in diameter (an even thickness is more important than a perfect circle). Lightly brush the tops with oil. Let the crusts sit at room temperature for 5 to 10 minutes.

**4.** Brush the cooking grate clean. Working with 1 or 2 crusts at a time, place the crusts on the cooking grate with the paper sides facing up. Grill over ***direct medium heat***, with the lid closed as much as possible, until the crusts are well marked and firm on the underside, 2 to 5 minutes, rotating the crusts for even cooking. Peel off and discard the parchment paper. Transfer the crusts to a work surface with the grilled sides facing up.

**5.** Working with 1 or 2 crusts at a time, spread ¼ to ⅓ cup of the sauce across the grilled side of each crust, leaving a ½-inch border around the edges. Arrange some sausage over the sauce. Sprinkle some of both cheeses on top. Transfer the pizzas to the cooking grate. Grill over ***direct medium heat***, with the lid closed as much as possible, until the cheese is melted and the bottom of the crusts are crisp, 2 to 5 minutes, rotating the pizzas occasionally for even cooking. Transfer to a cutting board. Brush the edges with oil, garnish with basil, and cut into wedges. Serve warm.

**Makes 8 small pizzas**

# ARTHUR SAMPSON

Arthur Sampson has lived in New England all his life and has eaten clams in almost every way imaginable, including of course at a traditional clambake. Legend has it that the clambake is a Native American tradition that European colonists adopted for their community events, in other words, as a seafood alternative to the smoky meat barbecues favored in the South. The method begins with digging a large pit in the sand, lining it with rocks, and heating the rocks with burning driftwood. After pushing the hot embers aside, you are meant to cover the rocks with damp seaweed and fill the pit with clams, lobsters, corn, potatoes, etc. Another layer of seaweed goes on top, followed by a tarp of some sort, to trap the steam and cook your dinner.

As the president and CEO of the Newport Hospital in Rhode Island, Arthur is usually too busy for such a time-consuming project. Instead, he has developed a decisively simpler method for cooking clams at the beach (or in his backyard). He arranges tender littleneck clams on a cooking grate above broiling hot coals. When the shells open, he showers the clams with beer from a spray bottle. "Just about anything will taste better if you put beer on it," Arthur suggests. Then it takes only a dip into some cocktail sauce or a splash of hot sauce to make this laid-back, delicious appetizer.

## Arthur's Beer-Showered Littleneck Clams

**Prep time: 5 minutes**
**Grilling time: about 8 minutes**

   4  dozen littleneck or manila clams
   1  cup beer (in a spray bottle)
   ½  cup good-quality cocktail sauce
      Tabasco® sauce

1. Prepare a two-zone fire for high heat (see pages 14-15).

2. Brush the cooking grate clean. Grill the clams over *direct high heat*, with the lid closed as much as possible, until some of the clams begin to open, 2 to 3 minutes. As they open, move the opened clams to the opposite side of the cooking grate, where no coals are directly underneath them. Spray the opened clams a few times with a little beer and keep them warm while the others cook over direct

heat. After 6 to 8 minutes, all the clams should be opened, moved to the other side of the cooking grate, and sprayed with beer. If any clams haven't opened after 8 minutes of cooking time, discard them (they are unsafe to eat).

3. Transfer the clams to a large bowl or platter. Spray them once more with beer. Serve right away with cocktail sauce and Tabasco® sauce.

**Makes 4 servings**

One note of caution: Before you start spraying the clams, move them to the side of the coals. Otherwise the beer may put out your fire.

# Grilled Oysters with Three Dipping Sauces

**Prep time: 30 minutes**
**Grilling time: 2 to 4 minutes for each batch**

### Latino sauce
¼ cup dry white wine
½ teaspoon finely grated lime zest
¼ cup fresh lime juice
1 tablespoon minced jalapeño chile pepper
1 tablespoon minced scallions
1 tablespoon minced fresh cilantro
1 teaspoon granulated sugar
¼ teaspoon kosher salt

### Mediterranean sauce
¼ cup dry white wine
½ teaspoon finely grated lemon zest
2 tablespoons fresh lemon juice
1 tablespoon minced shallot
2 teaspoons minced fresh oregano
½ teaspoon granulated sugar
½ teaspoon kosher salt
⅛ teaspoon red chile flakes

### Asian sauce
¼ cup fresh lime juice
1½ tablespoons minced chives
1 tablespoon rice wine vinegar
1 tablespoon soy sauce
2 teaspoons minced fresh ginger
1 teaspoon granulated sugar

24 large, fresh oysters

**1.** In 3 small bowls mix the sauces separately. Cover with plastic wrap and refrigerate for 1 to 2 hours before serving.

**2.** Grip each oyster, flat side up, in a folded kitchen towel. Find the small opening between the shells, near the hinge, and pry open with an oyster knife. Try to keep the juices in

1. Grip each oyster, flat side up, in a folded kitchen towel. Find the small opening between the shells, near the hinge, and pry open with an oyster knife.

2. Try not to spill the delicious juices, known as the "oyster liqueur," in the bottom shell.

the shell. Loosen the oyster from the shell by running the oyster knife carefully underneath the body. Discard the top, flatter shell, keeping the oyster and juices in the bottom, deeper shell.

**3.** Prepare a two-zone fire for high heat (see pages 14-15).

**4.** Grill the oysters in batches, shell sides down, over *direct high heat*, with the lid closed as much as possible, until the oyster juices start to steam and the edges curl, 2 to 4 minutes. Using tongs, carefully remove the oysters from the grill. Place the hot oysters on a platter with small bowls of the sauce for dipping the oysters. Serve with cocktail forks.

**Makes 4 to 6 servings**

> Big, meaty oysters tend to do better on the grill than smaller ones. After they have cooked in their own juices for a few minutes, they are still moist and briny.

# Mussels with Tomatoes, Scallions, Garlic, and Butter

**Prep time: 15 minutes**
**Grilling time: 6 to 8 minutes**

  2  large tomatoes, chopped into ½-inch pieces
  ½  cup thinly sliced scallions
  3  tablespoons unsalted butter, cut into 3 equal pieces
  1  tablespoon minced garlic
     Finely grated zest and juice of 1 lemon
  ¼  teaspoon crushed red pepper flakes
  ¼  teaspoon kosher salt
  ⅛  teaspoon freshly ground black pepper
  2  pounds live mussels, rinsed and debearded
  2  tablespoons finely chopped fresh Italian parsley
  1  baguette, torn into bite-size pieces

**1.** Prepare a two-zone fire for high heat (see pages 14-15).

**2.** In a 9 x 13-inch, heavy-duty foil pan combine the tomatoes, scallions, butter, garlic, lemon zest, lemon juice, red pepper flakes, salt, and pepper. Mix well. Scatter the mussels over the tomato mixture. Cover the pan with aluminum foil and crimp the edges to capture the steam.

**3.** Place the pan over ***direct high heat*** and cook, with the lid open, until the steam forces the shells open, 6 to 8 minutes. Discard any mussels that do not open within 10 minutes of cooking time (they are unsafe to eat).

Before cooking, yank the tuft of stringy hair, known as the "beard," toward the hinged end and remove it.

**4.** Carefully pour the mussels and all the liquid into a large serving bowl, toss gently with the parsley, and serve warm. Dip the pieces of bread into the liquid.

**Makes 4 servings**

# Smoked and Spiced Nuts

**Prep time: 5 minutes**
**Grilling time: 20 to 30 minutes**

  1  teaspoon light brown sugar
  1  teaspoon dried thyme or rosemary
     (or ½ teaspoon of each)
  ¼  teaspoon ground cayenne pepper
  ¼  teaspoon dry mustard powder
  2  cups mixed salted nuts
     (almonds, pecans, cashews, etc.)
  2  teaspoons extra virgin olive oil
  2  medium chunks hickory wood, soaked in water
     for at least 30 minutes

**1.** In a small bowl mix the sugar, thyme, cayenne, and mustard between your fingertips.

**2.** Pour the nuts into a 9 x 13-inch, heavy-duty foil pan. Add the oil and seasonings. Toss to coat the nuts evenly, and then spread them in a single layer.

**3.** Prepare a two-zone fire for low heat (see pages 14-15).

**4.** Place the chunks of hickory over the lit charcoal. When the chunks begin to smoke, place the pan of nuts over ***indirect low heat*** and cook, with the lid closed as much as possible, until the nuts are toasted and have a nice smoky flavor, 20 to 30 minutes, shaking the pan with tongs a couple times to prevent the nuts from burning. Using insulated mitts, remove the pan from the grill and let the nuts cool completely in the pan. The nuts will become crispier as they cool. Serve at room temperature. Store any remaining nuts in an airtight container.

**Makes 2 cups**

Mussels with Tomatoes, Scallions, Garlic, and Butter

A

Smoked and Spiced Nuts

RED MEAT

# Black Pepper New York Strip Steaks with Horseradish Sauce

**Prep time: 10 minutes**
**Grilling time: about 8 minutes**

**Sauce**
- ¾ cup sour cream
- 2 tablespoons prepared horseradish
- 2 tablespoons finely chopped fresh Italian parsley
- 2 teaspoons Dijon mustard
- 2 teaspoons Worcestershire sauce
- ½ teaspoon kosher salt
- ¼ teaspoon freshly ground black pepper

- 4 New York strip steaks, 10 to 12 ounces each and about 1 inch thick, trimmed of excess fat
- 2 tablespoons extra virgin olive oil
- 2 tablespoons Dijon mustard
- ¾ teaspoon kosher salt
- ¾ teaspoon freshly ground black pepper

**1.** In a medium bowl thoroughly mix the sauce ingredients.

**2.** Prepare a two-zone fire for high heat (see pages 14-15).

**3.** Lightly brush the steaks on both sides with the oil, and then smear the mustard on both sides. Season evenly with the salt and pepper. Let the steaks sit at room temperature for 20 to 30 minutes before grilling.

**4.** Brush the cooking grate clean. Sear the steaks over **direct high heat**, with the lid closed as much as possible, for about 6 minutes, turning once and swapping their positions as needed for even cooking. Move the steaks over **indirect high heat** and cook, with the lid closed, until they reach your desired doneness, about 2 minutes for medium rare. Remove from the grill and let the steaks rest for 3 to 5 minutes. Serve the steaks warm with the sauce on the side.

**Makes 4 servings**

## Checking for Doneness

An instant-read thermometer will reliably tell you the doneness of a steak if its sensor is right in the middle. Otherwise use the "touch test," which gauges doneness by the firmness of a steak. Your last resort is to cut open the underside of a steak and judge doneness by the color of the meat.

# New York Strip Steaks with Red-Eye Barbecue Sauce

**Prep time: 15 minutes**
**Grilling time: 8 to 10 minutes**

**Sauce**
½ cup ketchup
½ cup low-sodium beef stock
¼ cup strong brewed coffee
1 tablespoon Worcestershire sauce
1 teaspoon molasses
½ teaspoon pure chile powder
½ teaspoon granulated onion
¼ teaspoon freshly ground black pepper
¼ teaspoon kosher salt

3 tablespoons vegetable oil
1 tablespoon Worcestershire sauce
1 tablespoon red wine vinegar
1 tablespoon freshly ground black pepper
2 teaspoons kosher salt
4 New York strip steaks, each about 12 ounces
   and 1¼ inches thick, trimmed of excess fat

1. In a small saucepan mix the sauce ingredients with ¼ cup water. Bring to a boil over high heat, then reduce the heat to a simmer and cook for 5 to 7 minutes, stirring occasionally. Remove the saucepan from the heat.

2. Prepare a two-zone fire for high heat (see pages 14-15), using mesquite lump charcoal.

3. In a small bowl mix the oil, Worcestershire sauce, vinegar, pepper, and salt. Brush the mixture over both sides of the steaks. Let the steaks sit at room temperature for 20 to 30 minutes before grilling.

4. Brush the cooking grate clean. Sear the steaks over *direct high heat*, with the lid closed as much as possible, for about 6 minutes, turning once and swapping their positions as needed for even cooking. Move the steaks over *indirect high heat* and cook, with the lid closed as much as possible, until they reach your desired doneness, 2 to 4 minutes for medium rare, occasionally turning and brushing with some of the sauce. Remove from the grill and let the steaks rest for 3 to 5 minutes. Serve warm with the remaining sauce.

**Makes 4 to 6 servings**

# Rosemary-Crusted Porterhouse Steaks with Red Wine Sauce

**Prep time: 20 to 30 minutes**
**Grilling time: 10 to 12 minutes**

**Sauce**
    2   cups low-sodium beef stock
    1   cup dry red wine
   ½   cup ketchup
   ¼   teaspoon dried thyme
   ¼   teaspoon freshly ground black pepper

    2   porterhouse steaks, 1 to 1¼ pounds each
        and about 1¼ inches thick, trimmed of excess fat
        Extra virgin olive oil
    2   tablespoons finely chopped fresh rosemary
    2   teaspoons kosher salt
    1   teaspoon freshly ground black pepper
    2   tablespoons unsalted butter, cut into 2 equal pieces

**1.** In a medium saucepan whisk the beef stock, wine, ketchup, thyme, and pepper. Bring the mixture to a boil over medium-high heat, then reduce the heat to a simmer and cook until about 1 cup remains, 20 to 30 minutes, stirring occasionally. Remove the saucepan from the heat.

**2.** Prepare a two-zone fire for high heat (see pages 14-15).

**3.** Lightly coat the steaks on both sides with oil. Season evenly with the rosemary, salt, and pepper. Let sit at room temperature for 20 to 30 minutes before grilling.

**4.** Brush the cooking grate clean. Sear the steaks over *direct high heat*, with the lid closed as much as possible, for about 6 minutes, turning once and swapping their positions as needed for even cooking. Then move the steaks over *indirect high heat* and cook to your desired doneness, 4 to 6 minutes for medium rare. By rotating the steaks so the tenderloin section is facing away from the hot fire, you will protect that meat from overcooking. Remove the steaks from the grill and let rest for 3 to 5 minutes.

**5.** Bring the sauce to a simmer. Add the butter and whisk to incorporate it. If necessary, adjust the seasonings. Carve the steaks and serve warm with the sauce.

**Makes 4 servings**

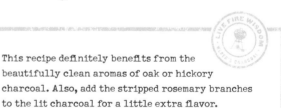

This recipe definitely benefits from the beautifully clean aromas of oak or hickory charcoal. Also, add the stripped rosemary branches to the lit charcoal for a little extra flavor.

# T-Bones with Avocado Salsa

**Prep time: 20 minutes**
**Grilling time: 10 to 12 minutes**

**Salsa**
- 2 ripe Haas avocados, finely diced or mashed
- 1 cup finely diced tomato
- 4 scallions, white and light green parts, finely chopped
- 2 tablespoon fresh lime juice
- 2 tablespoons finely chopped fresh basil
- 1 tablespoon extra virgin olive oil
- 1 teaspoon minced garlic
- 1 teaspoon minced jalapeño chile pepper
- ¾ teaspoon kosher salt
- ¼ teaspoon Worcestershire sauce
- ¼ teaspoon freshly ground black pepper

- 2 tablespoons roughly chopped garlic
- 2 teaspoons kosher salt, divided
- 2 T-bone steaks, 1 to 1¼ pounds each and about 1¼ inches thick, trimmed of excess fat
  Extra virgin olive oil
- 1 teaspoon freshly ground black pepper

**1.** In a medium bowl mix the salsa ingredients. Set aside at room temperature for up to 2 hours before serving.

**2.** Make a little pile of the garlic on a cutting board. Sprinkle about 1 teaspoon of salt over the garlic. Finely chop the garlic and use the side of the knife to crush the garlic and salt into a paste (see photo above).

**3.** Prepare a two-zone fire for high heat (see pages 14-15).

Kosher salt works as an abrasive that helps the side of the knife break down garlic into a paste.

**4.** Lightly coat the steaks on both sides with oil. Smear the garlic paste over both sides. Season evenly with the remaining 1 teaspoon of salt and the pepper. Let sit at room temperature for 20 to 30 minutes before grilling.

**5.** Brush the cooking grate clean. Sear the steaks over *direct high heat*, with the lid closed as much as possible, for about 6 minutes, turning once and swapping their positions as needed for even cooking. Then move the steaks over *indirect high heat* and cook to your desired doneness, 4 to 6 minutes for medium rare. By rotating the steaks so the tenderloin section is facing away from the hot fire, you will protect that meat from overcooking. Remove the steaks from the grill and let rest for 3 to 5 minutes.

**6.** Carve the steaks. Serve warm with the salsa.

**Makes 4 servings**

# Filet Mignon Steaks with Martini Marinade

**Prep time: 10 minutes**
**Marinating time: 1 to 2 hours**
**Grilling time: 8 to 10 minutes**

**Marinade**
2 tablespoons gin
2 tablespoons extra virgin olive oil
1 tablespoon juice from a jar of green olives
   Grated zest of 1 lemon
¼ teaspoon freshly ground black pepper

4 filet mignon steaks, each about 8 ounces
   and 1¼ inches thick
8 green olives stuffed with pimentos
   (or 4 green olives and 4 cocktail onions)
4 toothpicks
½ teaspoon kosher salt
½ teaspoon freshly ground black pepper
2 ounces blue cheese

**1.** In a small bowl whisk the marinade ingredients.

**2.** Place the steaks in a large, plastic resealable bag and pour in the marinade. Press the air out of the bag and seal tightly. Turn the bag to distribute the marinade, place in a bowl, and refrigerate for 1 to 2 hours.

**3.** Skewer 2 olives (or 1 olive and 1 onion) onto each toothpick.

**4.** Prepare a two-zone fire for high heat (see pages 14-15).

**5.** Remove the steaks from the bag, letting the liquid drip away. Discard the marinade. Let the steaks sit at room temperature for 20 to 30 minutes before grilling. Season evenly with the salt and pepper. Brush the cooking grate clean. Grill the steaks over ***direct high heat***, with the lid closed as much as possible, until cooked to your desired doneness, 8 to 10 minutes for medium rare, turning once and swapping their positions as needed for even cooking. Remove the steaks from the grill and let rest for 3 to 5 minutes. Crumble the blue cheese over the top. Serve warm with a skewer of olives poked in the middle of each steak.

**Makes 4 servings**

# Lemon-Sage Marinated Veal Chops

**Prep time: 15 minutes**
**Marinating time: 8 to 12 hours**
**Grilling time: 8 to 12 minutes**

**Marinade**
 1  tablespoon finely grated lemon zest
 ¼  cup fresh lemon juice
 ¼  cup extra virgin olive oil
 3  tablespoons finely chopped fresh sage
 2  tablespoons minced shallot
 2  tablespoons whole grain mustard
 1  tablespoon finely chopped garlic
 1  tablespoon freshly cracked black peppercorns

 4  veal rib chops (with bone), 8 to 10 ounces each
    and 1 to 1¼ inches thick
 1  teaspoon kosher salt
    Lemon slices
    Fresh sage leaves, optional

**1.** In a large, resealable plastic bag combine the marinade ingredients. Place the chops in the bag. Press the air out of the bag and seal tightly. Turn the bag several times to distribute the marinade, place the bag in a bowl, and refrigerate for 8 to 12 hours, turning occasionally.

**2.** Remove the chops from the bag. Discard the marinade. Season the chops evenly with the salt. Let the chops sit at room temperature for 20 to 30 minutes before grilling.

**3.** Prepare a two-zone fire for high heat (see pages 14-15).

**4.** Brush the cooking grate clean. Sear the chops over *direct high heat*, with the lid closed as much as possible, 4 to 6 minutes, turning once and swapping their positions as needed for even cooking. Then grill the chops over *indirect high heat*, with the lid closed as much as possible, until cooked to your desired doneness, 4 to 6 minutes for medium rare, turning once. During the last 2 minutes of grilling time, grill the lemon slices, one side only, over *direct high heat*, until slightly charred and softened. Remove from the grill and let the chops rest for 3 to 5 minutes. Garnish with the grilled lemon slices and fresh sage leaves, if desired. Serve warm.

**Makes 4 servings**

# MIKE McGRATH

Mike McGrath of Woodbury, Minnesota, used this recipe to win a grilling competition at Chicago's Backyard Barbecue in 2005. Since then so many friends and family members have asked him for his award-winning rub that he mixes all the ingredients, except the fresh garlic, in huge batches. He gives away the rub with a simple direction: Just add garlic.

Mike's rub is terrific, but his technique is equally as important to the flavor and tenderness of his steaks. First of all, he always lets the steaks sit at room temperature for 20 to 30 minutes before grilling. This shortens the cooking time. In other words, the interior of each steak reaches his desired doneness faster, so there is less chance of overcooking the exterior. Mike also displays an experienced grill jockey's responsiveness. He is quick to move any steak that is threatened by flare-ups. And to compensate for any unevenness in the fire, he swaps the positions of the steaks so they all get the searing heat they need.

## Mike's Rib-Eyes with Award-Winning Rub

**Prep time: 5 minutes**
**Grilling time: 8 to 10 minutes**

**Rub**
- 4 teaspoons coarse kosher salt
- 1 tablespoon coarsely ground black pepper
- 1 teaspoon dried oregano
- 1 teaspoon dried thyme
- 1 teaspoon paprika
- 1 teaspoon minced garlic

- 6 boneless rib-eye steaks, about 12 ounces each and 1 to 1¼ inches thick, trimmed of excess fat
  Vegetable oil

**1.** Prepare a two-zone fire for high heat (see pages 14-15), using enough charcoal so that all 6 steaks can cook over direct heat.

**2.** In a small bowl mix the rub ingredients. Lightly coat the steaks with oil. Massage the rub into both sides of each steak. Let the steaks sit at room temperature for 20 to 30 minutes before grilling.

**3.** Brush the cooking grate clean. Grill the steaks over ***direct high heat***, with the lid closed as much as possible, until cooked to your desired doneness, 8 to 10 minutes for medium rare, rotating each steak 90 degrees halfway through each side and swapping their positions as needed for even cooking. If flare-ups occur, move the steaks temporarily over indirect heat. Remove from the grill, tent loosely with foil, and let rest for 3 to 5 minutes. Serve warm.

**Makes 6 servings**

# Coffee-Crusted Rib-Eye Steaks

**Prep time: 5 minutes**
**Grilling time: 6 to 8 minutes**

**Rub**
- 1 tablespoon finely ground dark-roasted coffee
- 2 teaspoons kosher salt
- 1 teaspoon light brown sugar
- ½ teaspoon freshly ground black pepper
- ¼ teaspoon ground allspice, optional

- 4 boneless rib-eye steaks, 8 to 10 ounces each and about 1 inch thick, trimmed of excess fat
  Extra virgin olive oil

**1.** In a small bowl mix the rub ingredients.

**2.** Prepare a two-zone fire for high heat (see pages 14-15).

**3.** Lightly coat the steaks on both sides with oil. Season evenly with the rub. Let the steaks sit at room temperature for 20 to 30 minutes before grilling.

**4.** Brush the cooking grate clean. Grill the steaks over **direct high heat**, with the lid closed as much as possible, until well marked on each side, 4 to 5 minutes, turning once and swapping their positions as needed for even cooking. Finish cooking the steaks over **indirect high heat**, with the lid closed, until they reach your desired doneness, 2 to 3 minutes for medium rare, turning once. Remove from the grill and let rest for 3 to 5 minutes. Serve warm.

Holding up a steak to sear the fat on the perimeter creates great flavors all around.

**Makes 4 servings**

# Spice-Rubbed Rib-Eye Kabobs with Salsa Verde

**Prep time: 20 minutes**
**Grilling time: 4 to 6 minutes**

**Rub**
2  teaspoons kosher salt
1  teaspoon light brown sugar
½  teaspoon freshly ground black pepper
½  teaspoon granulated garlic
½  teaspoon prepared chili powder

4  boneless rib-eye steaks, about 12 ounces each
   and 1 to 1½ inches thick
   Extra virgin olive oil
12  wooden skewers, soaked in water for
   at least 30 minutes

**Sauce**
½  cup tightly packed fresh basil leaves and tender stems
½  cup tightly packed fresh Italian parsley leaves
   and tender stems
2  anchovy fillets
1  medium garlic clove
6  tablespoons extra virgin olive oil
1  tablespoon red wine vinegar
1  teaspoon finely chopped jalapeño chile pepper,
   without seeds
¼  teaspoon kosher salt
⅛  teaspoon freshly ground black pepper

**1.** In a large bowl mix the rub ingredients.

**2.** Cut the rib-eye steaks into chunks 1 to 1½ inches thick, removing and discarding any large pieces of fat. Add the chunks of steak to the bowl and toss to coat them evenly with the rub. Add just enough oil to lightly coat the chunks of meat. Mix well. Thread the chunks onto skewers, leaving a little room between each chunk. Set aside at room temperature for 20 to 30 minutes before grilling.

**3.** Prepare a two-zone fire for high heat (see pages 14-15).

**4.** In a food processor finely chop the basil, parsley, anchovy fillets, and garlic. Add the remaining sauce ingredients and let the machine run until the sauce is well combined, 1 to 2 minutes, scraping down the sides of the bowl occasionally.

**5.** Brush the cooking grate clean. Grill the skewers over *direct high heat*, with the lid closed as much as possible, until cooked to your desired doneness, 4 to 6 minutes for medium rare, turning once or twice and swapping their positions as needed for even cooking. Serve warm with the sauce.

**Makes 4 to 6 servings**

# Yakiniku

**Prep time: 25 minutes**
**Freezer time: 2 hours**
**Grilling time: about 4 minutes**

  1  boneless rib roast, about 3 pounds

**Pickles**
¼  cup rice vinegar
 1  tablespoon fresh lemon juice
 1  tablespoon granulated sugar
 1  teaspoon kosher salt
 2  thin Japanese cucumbers, 4 to 6 ounces each

**Sauce**
¼  cup white miso
¼  cup mirin (sweet rice wine)
 3  tablespoons soy sauce
 1  tablespoon fresh lemon juice
 2  teaspoons granulated sugar
¼  teaspoon freshly ground black pepper

 1  teaspoon kosher salt
½  teaspoon freshly ground black pepper
 6  cups steamed white rice

**1.** In order to cut the meat into thin slices, wrap the roast in plastic or paper and place in the freezer for about 2 hours.

**2.** In a medium bowl mix the vinegar, lemon juice, sugar, and salt until the sugar and salt are dissolved. Add ¼ cup of water. Trim the ends of the cucumbers and discard. Cut the cucumbers into thin strips, each about ¼ inch wide and 3 inches long (could be any shape, really). Add the cucumbers to the pickling liquid and set aside at room temperature for 2 hours, stirring the cucumbers a few times. Drain the pickles before serving.

**3.** In a medium bowl combine the sauce ingredients with ¼ cup water. Whisk until the miso is dissolved. Divide the sauce into individual dipping bowls.

**4.** When the meat is cold and hard, cut it crosswise into ¼-inch slices. Lay the slices flat on sheet pans and let sit at room temperature for 20 to 30 minutes before grilling.

**5.** Prepare a two-zone fire for high heat (see pages 14-15).

**6.** Just before grilling, season the meat slices evenly with the salt and pepper. Brush the cooking grate clean. Grill the meat slices in 2 batches over ***direct high heat***, with the lid open, until medium rare, about 2 minutes, turning once or twice. After both batches are cooked, cut the meat into strips about 1 inch wide. The meat strips may go onto a large platter to be served family style along with individual bowls of rice, dipping sauce, and pickles.

**Makes 4 to 6 servings**

# Grill-Roasted Prime Rib Au Jus

**Prep time: 15 minutes**
**Grilling time: 2½ to 3 hours**

- 1 bone-in prime rib roast (with 4 bones), about 8 pounds
- 3 large garlic cloves
- 1 tablespoon kosher salt
- 1 teaspoon freshly ground black pepper
- 2 large handfuls oak wood chips, soaked in water for at least 30 minutes

**1.** Stand the roast on its side and remove the rib bones (see photos below).

**2.** Trim any excess surface fat to a thickness of ¼ inch. Thinly slice the garlic cloves. Using a sharp knife, make little slits in the fat and slip in the garlic slices. Slip in garlic slices wherever you can but don't use a knife to cut slits in the meat, as that would let precious juices escape during cooking. Season evenly with the salt and pepper. Tie the bones back onto the roast with kitchen twine (see photo below). Let the roast sit at room temperature for 1 to 1½ hours before grilling.

**3.** Prepare a two-zone fire for medium heat (see pages 14-15). Place a large, disposable drip pan on the empty side of the charcoal grate and fill it about halfway with warm water.

**4.** Brush the cooking grate clean. Sear the roast over ***direct medium heat***, with the lid closed as much as possible, until golden brown on all sides except the cut ends, 8 to 10 minutes, turning every few minutes. If flare-ups occur, temporarily move the roast over indirect heat until the flames die down.

**5.** When the roast is well browned, move it to indirect heat, with the bone side facing down. Drain the oak chips and drop them right onto the charcoal so they smoke. Close the lid and cook the roast over ***indirect low heat*** until it reaches your desired doneness, 2½ to 3 hours for medium rare (125°F), rotating the roast once or twice for even cooking. Replenish the charcoal as needed to maintain indirect low heat, adding 8 to 10 unlit charcoal briquettes to the lit charcoal every 30 to 45 minutes. The roast should finish cooking at a much lower temperature than where it started. Begin checking the internal temperature of the roast after 2 hours.

**6.** Remove the roast from the grill, wrap in aluminum foil, and let rest for 20 to 30 minutes. During resting, the roast's internal temperature will continue to rise 5°F to 10°F and the juices will redistribute themselves evenly throughout.

**7.** Unwrap the roast, being careful to capture the meat juices in the bottom of the foil. Pour the juices into a small bowl. Untie the roast and remove the bones. Cut the meat crosswise into slices. Arrange on a platter or individual plates. Spoon the juices over the meat.

**Makes 6 to 8 servings**

Sear the roast on both sides over direct heat. Finish the roast, bone side down, over indirect heat.

If you remove the bones from the meat and then reattach them with twine before cooking, the meat will absorb the flavors of the bones and slicing later will be easy. 1. Stand the roast on its side, with the ribs facing up. 2. Use a large knife to cut as close to the ribs as possible. 3. Completely separate the ribs from the meat. 4. With a small knife, make little slits in the fat. 5. Slip in thin slices of garlic. 6. Place the ribs back in their original position and secure them with kitchen twine.

# Family Fajita Bar

**Prep time: 30 minutes**
**Marinating time: 1 to 2 hours**
**Grilling time: 18 to 23 minutes**

### Guacamole

- 4  ripe Haas avocados, mashed
- 2  tablespoons finely chopped fresh cilantro or basil
- 1½  tablespoons fresh lime juice
- 1  teaspoon kosher salt
- ¼  teaspoon freshly ground black pepper

### Marinade

- 3  large garlic cloves
- ½  cup loosely packed fresh cilantro or basil
- ¼  cup fresh orange juice
- 3  tablespoons extra virgin olive oil
- 1  tablespoon fresh lime juice
- 2  teaspoons pure chile powder
- 1  teaspoon dry mustard
- 1  teaspoon dried oregano
- 1  teaspoon kosher salt
- 1  teaspoon ground cumin
- ½  teaspoon ground coriander

- 1½  pounds flank steak, about ¾ inch thick
- 1½  pounds boneless, skinless chicken thighs
- 4  medium green bell peppers, seeded and cut into flat sections
- 2  medium red onions, sliced crosswise into ⅓-inch slices
  Extra virgin olive oil
- 10  flour tortillas (9 to 10 inches)
- 2  cups good-quality, store-bought chunky salsa
  Tabasco® sauce

**1.** In a medium bowl combine the guacamole ingredients and stir with a fork until thoroughly combined. Cover the surface with plastic wrap until ready to use.

**2.** In a blender or food processor finely chop the garlic and cilantro. Add the remaining marinade ingredients. Process until smooth.

**3.** Put the flank steak in one medium bowl and the chicken thighs in another. Add half the marinade to the steak and half to the chicken and toss to evenly coat all sides. Cover and refrigerate for 1 to 2 hours.

**4.** Prepare a two-zone fire for medium heat (see pages 14-15).

**5.** Lightly coat the bell peppers and onions on both sides with oil. Brush the cooking grate clean. Grill them over ***direct medium heat***, with the lid closed as much as possible, until tender, turning once and swapping their positions as needed for even cooking. The bell peppers will take 6 to 8 minutes and the onions will take 8 to 10 minutes. Cut the bell peppers and onions into ⅓-inch strips.

**6.** Remove the steak and chicken from their bowls and discard the marinade. Grill them over ***direct medium heat***, with the lid closed as much as possible, until the steak is medium rare and the chicken is brown on the surface and no longer pink in the middle, 8 to 10 minutes, turning once and swapping their positions as needed for even cooking. Let the steak rest for 2 to 3 minutes. Evenly divide the tortillas into 2 foil packets and grill over ***direct medium heat*** to warm them, 2 to 3 minutes, turning once.

**7.** Cut the steak in half lengthwise, and then cut crosswise into ¼-inch slices. Cut the chicken into ¼-inch slices. Place the tortillas, steak, chicken, peppers, onions, guacamole, and salsa in separate serving dishes. Let each person make their own fajita by placing the fillings down the center of each tortilla and adding Tabasco® sauce to taste. Serve warm.

**Makes 8 to 10 servings**

# Mesquite-Grilled Flank Steak with Black Bean Salad

**Prep time: 25 minutes**
**Grilling time: 8 to 10 minutes**

**Rub**
1 teaspoon pure chile powder
1 teaspoon ground cumin
1 teaspoon dried oregano
1 teaspoon kosher salt
½ teaspoon freshly ground black pepper
⅛ teaspoon ground cinnamon, optional

**Salad**
1 can (15 ounces) black beans, rinsed
1 cup seeded, finely diced tomatoes
½ cup ¼-inch-diced yellow bell pepper
⅓ cup ¼-inch-diced red onion
⅓ cup thinly sliced scallions, white and light green parts
2 tablespoons extra virgin olive oil
1 tablespoon fresh lime juice
1 teaspoon minced garlic

1 flank steak, 1½ to 2 pounds and about ¾ inch thick
Extra virgin olive oil
Kosher salt
Freshly ground black pepper

**1.** In a small bowl mix the rub ingredients.

**2.** In a medium bowl combine the salad ingredients, including ¾ teaspoon of the rub. Mix gently but thoroughly. If desired, to let the flavors meld, set aside at room temperature for at least 1 hour or as long as 8 hours.

**3.** Prepare a two-zone fire for high heat (see pages 14-15), using mesquite lump charcoal.

**4.** Lightly coat the steak with oil. Season evenly with the remaining rub. Let the steak sit at room temperature for 20 to 30 minutes before grilling.

**5.** Brush the cooking grate clean. Grill the steak over *direct high heat*, with the lid closed as much as possible, until cooked to your desired doneness, 8 to 10 minutes for medium rare, turning once and rotating as needed for even cooking. Remove from the grill and let rest for 3 to 5 minutes. Season the salad with salt and pepper to taste.

**6.** Cut the steak against the grain into ¼-inch slices. The thinner the slices, the more tender the meat will be. Serve the meat warm along with the juices on the cutting board and the black bean salad.

**Makes 4 servings**

# Steak Salad with Tarragon-Mustard Vinaigrette

**Prep time: 10 minutes**

  1  pound leftover grilled steak, preferably flatiron, flank, or skirt steak

**Vinaigrette**

  1  teaspoon minced garlic
  1  teaspoon finely grated fresh ginger
1½  tablespoons rice wine vinegar
 ½  teaspoon kosher salt
  1  tablespoon Dijon mustard
  1  tablespoon chopped fresh tarragon
 ½  cup extra virgin olive oil

  8  cups mixed fresh greens (romaine, arugula, radicchio, or any combination)
 ½  cup thinly sliced red onion
  8  sprigs fresh tarragon leaves, stems discarded
  1  cup (6 ounces) crumbled goat cheese

**1.** Remove the steak from the refrigerator about 30 minutes before serving. Cut away all the fat and thinly slice the steak across the grain on the bias.

**2.** In a medium bowl combine the garlic, ginger, vinegar, and salt, and set aside for 5 to 10 minutes. Then whisk in

the mustard and tarragon. While whisking, slowly drizzle in the olive oil to make an emulsion (see photo above).

**3.** In a large bowl toss the greens with 2 or 3 tablespoons of the dressing. Arrange the greens on separate plates and distribute the onion and tarragon leaves over the greens. Arrange the steak slices on top of each salad, and spoon some vinaigrette over the meat (you may not need all of it). Sprinkle the cheese on top.

**Makes 4 servings**

# Pepper Steak Tacos with Pico de Gallo

**Prep time: 15 minutes**
**Grilling time: 5 to 7 minutes**

### Salsa
  2  cups seeded, finely diced ripe tomato
  1  cup ¼-inch-diced red onion
  3  tablespoons finely chopped fresh cilantro
  2  tablespoons fresh lime juice
  1  teaspoon minced serrano chile
  ¾  teaspoon kosher salt

### Rub
  1½  teaspoons whole black peppercorns
  1½  teaspoons cumin seed
  1½  teaspoons kosher salt
  ¾  teaspoon pure chile powder
  ¾  teaspoon granulated garlic

  1½  pounds skirt steak, about ½ inch thick,
      trimmed of excess surface fat
      Extra virgin olive oil
  12  corn or flour tortillas (6 to 8 inches)

**1.** In a medium bowl combine the salsa ingredients. Mix well. If desired, to fully incorporate the flavors, let the salsa sit at room temperature for 1 hour.

**2.** Using a mortar and pestle or spice mill, crush the peppercorns and the cumin seed. Place in a small bowl and mix with the remaining rub ingredients.

**3.** Prepare a two-zone fire for high heat (see pages 14-15), using mesquite lump charcoal.

**4.** Cut the skirt steak into 2 or 3 sections so they fit on the grill. Lightly coat each of the steaks with oil. Season them evenly with the rub. Let the steaks sit at room temperature for 20 to 30 minutes before grilling. Stack 6 tortillas on top of each other and wrap them in aluminum foil. Repeat with the remaining 6 tortillas.

**5.** Brush the cooking grate clean. Grill the steaks over ***direct high heat***, with the lid closed as much as possible, until lightly charred on the surface and cooked to your desired doneness, 5 to 7 minutes for medium rare, turning once or twice and swapping their positions as needed for even cooking. At the same time, warm the 2 packets of tortillas over ***indirect high heat*** for 4 to 6 minutes, turning once. Remove the steaks and tortillas from the grill and let the steaks rest for 2 to 3 minutes (keep the tortillas warm in the foil). Cut the meat across the grain into thin slices. Pile the meat inside warm tortillas and top with the salsa, draining the juices back into the bowl so the tortillas don't get too wet. Serve immediately.

**Makes 4 servings**

The medium spiciness in this pico de gallo salsa comes mostly from the seeds and veins inside serrano chiles.

# JIM MINION

Jim Minion is a board member of the Kansas City Barbeque Society, which is the sanctioning body for many of America's most prestigious competitions. He is also a very successful cook, with several ribbons and trophies to show for his prodigious talent. Yet Jim may be best known for a particular way of cooking with a Weber® Smokey Mountain Cooker™ smoker. His "Minion Method" eliminates the need to replenish charcoal for as long as twenty hours, which has been a big boon to barbecue competitors who start smoking their briskets on Friday night and like to get some sleep that night before turning in their meat to the judges on Saturday afternoon. It is detailed in the recipe on the following page.

Conventional wisdom says that if you cook a brisket with the fat side facing up, the fat will melt slowly and seep into the meat, making it moist and delicious. Jim begs to differ. He claims the fat on top can't possibly penetrate the meat and that the only moisture you are going to get is already inside the meat. Actually it is inside the connective tissue. When the tissue reaches an internal temperature of 160°F, it melts and releases its moisture into the meat. So you are better off cooking brisket with the fat side down, Jim says, to protect the meat from the heat rising from the bottom of the smoker.

On the top side of a brisket leave all the soft fat in place. On the underside, remove the hard fat near one end.

A well-balanced spice rub not only seasons the meat, it cures it, too, helping to develop a savory crust around each succulent slice.

# Jim's All-Night Brisket

**Prep time: 20 minutes**
**Grilling time: 10 to 15 hours**
**Resting time: 2 to 4 hours**

1 brisket, 8 to 10 pounds

**Rub**

2 tablespoons granulated sugar
2 tablespoons ground black pepper
2 tablespoons sweet paprika
2 tablespoons pure chile powder
2 teaspoons onion salt
2 teaspoons garlic salt
2 teaspoons celery salt
2 teaspoons seasoning salt

3 fist-size dry chunks apple, cherry, oak,
or mesquite wood (not soaked)

1. Lay the brisket, fat side down, on a work surface. Trim the hard fat near the pointed end and remove the tough membrane on the surface of the meat (see page 238).

2. In a medium bowl mix the rub ingredients. Season the brisket evenly with the rub. Wrap the seasoned brisket in plastic wrap and refrigerate until ready to cook.

3. Using a Weber® Smokey Mountain Cooker™ smoker, fill the bottom ring with one chimney starter full of unlit charcoal briquettes. Then light 15 to 20 charcoal briquettes in the chimney starter. When they are burning with flames, pour them carefully over the top of the unlit charcoal. Add the wood chunks. Open the bottom vents completely.

4. Place the center section of the smoker on the bottom section, add the water pan, fill the pan with water, and put the cooking grates in place. Brush the top cooking grate clean. Place the brisket, fat side down, on the top cooking grate. *Note: The reason for taking the brisket straight from the refrigerator to the smoker is to help produce an attractive smoke ring. Once the internal temperature of the brisket reaches 140°F, the smoke ring will not develop anymore.* Put the lid on the smoker with the top vent completely open. Place a thermometer in one of the holes in the top vent to keep track of the temperature. Close

the bottom vents about halfway. The temperature in the smoker will begin to fall. As it approaches 250°F, close the bottom vents three-quarters of the way.

5. Brisket takes approximately 1¼ to 1½ hours per pound (roughly 10 to 15 hours), but the internal temperature is the most important indicator of doneness. It should reach 190°F in the thickest section. You should not need to add charcoal to the smoker. Just adjust the bottom vents periodically to maintain the temperature between 225°F and 250°F. During the second half of cooking time, refill the water pan with warm water, if necessary.

6. When the internal temperature of the brisket reaches 190°F in the thickest section, remove it from the smoker and tightly wrap it in 2 layers of heavy-duty foil. Place the wrapped brisket in a dry cooler (no ice or liquid) to rest for 2 to 4 hours. While in the dry cooler, the brisket will continue to tenderize. The brisket will stay hot in the cooler during this time.

7. When you are ready to serve, carefully unwrap the brisket, reserving the precious juices. Pour into a bowl for serving. Slide a long knife between the top and bottom sections to separate those two muscles. Trim the excess fat from both sections and slice the meat of the bottom section across the grain. To serve the top section, chop it into small pieces. Serve the brisket warm with the juices.

**Makes 8 to 10 servings**

# Porcini Burgers with Tomato and Pesto

**Prep time: 15 minutes**
**Grilling time: 8 to 10 minutes**

- ½ cup dried porcini mushroom pieces, about ½ ounce total
- 1½ pounds ground chuck (80% lean)
- 2 teaspoons minced garlic
- 1 teaspoon kosher salt
- ½ teaspoon freshly ground black pepper
- ½ teaspoon balsamic vinegar
- ⅓ cup mayonnaise
- 2 tablespoons prepared basil pesto
- 4 hamburger buns
- 1 cup shaved (chiffonade) green or red lettuce
- 1 ripe tomato, cut into ¼-inch slices

**1.** In a small saucepan bring about 2 cups of water to a boil. Add the dried mushroom pieces, mix briefly, remove the saucepan from the heat, and let the mushrooms soak until soft, about 30 minutes. Drain the mushrooms and gently squeeze out the excess water. Finely chop them, discarding any tough stems.

**2.** In a medium bowl gently combine the ground chuck with the mushrooms, garlic, salt, pepper, and vinegar until the ingredients are evenly distributed. Gently shape the meat into 4 patties of equal size and thickness, about ¾ inch thick. With your fingertips or thumb, make a shallow depression about 1 inch wide in the center of each patty so the centers are about ½ inch thick (see page 89). This will help the patties cook evenly and prevent them from puffing on the grill.

**3.** In a small bowl mix the mayonnaise and pesto.

Dried porcini mushrooms turn soft and delicious after 30 minutes in hot water.

**4.** Prepare a two-zone fire for high heat (see pages 14-15).

**5.** Brush the cooking grate clean. Grill the patties over *direct high heat*, with the lid closed as much as possible, until cooked to medium, 8 to 10 minutes, turning once when the patties release easily from the grate without sticking, and swapping their positions as needed for even cooking. Move the patties over indirect heat to keep them warm. With the lid open, grill the buns, cut sides down, over direct heat until toasted, 20 to 30 seconds.

**6.** Lightly brush the bottom of each bun with some of the mayonnaise mixture. Place the lettuce and tomato slices on top. Put the patties on top of the tomatoes and spread the remaining mayonnaise on top. Crown the burgers with the tops of each bun and serve warm.

**Makes 4 servings**

# Jalapeño and Avocado Cheeseburgers

**Prep time: 15 minutes**
**Grilling time: 10 to 12 minutes**

 2  pounds ground chuck (80% lean)
 ¼  cup coarsely grated red onion
 3  tablespoons finely chopped fresh Italian parsley
    or cilantro
 2  teaspoons minced jalapeño chile pepper, with seeds
 1½ teaspoons kosher salt
 ½  teaspoon granulated garlic
 ¼  teaspoon freshly ground black pepper
 1  ripe Haas avocado
 4  thin slices pepper Jack cheese
 4  hamburger buns
 4  lettuce leaves, optional

**1.** In a medium bowl gently combine the ground chuck with the red onion, parsley, jalapeño, salt, granulated garlic, and pepper. Gently shape the mixture into 4 patties of equal size and thickness, ¾ to 1 inch thick. With your fingertips or thumb, make a shallow depression about 1 inch wide in the center of each patty so the centers are about ½ inch thick. This will help the patties cook evenly and prevent them from puffing on the grill.

**2.** Cut the avocado in half lengthwise, remove the pit, and peel. Cut lengthwise into ¼-inch slices.

**3.** Prepare a two-zone fire for high heat (see pages 14-15).

**4.** Brush the cooking grate clean. Grill the patties over ***direct high heat***, with the lid closed as much as possible, until cooked to medium, 10 to 12 minutes, turning once

Dimpling the patty prevents it from puffing up on the grill.

when the patties release easily from the grate without sticking, and swapping their positions as needed for even cooking. During the last minute of grilling time place a slice of cheese on each patty to melt, and grill the buns, cut sides down, over direct heat until toasted, 20 to 30 seconds. Assemble the cheeseburgers with the avocado and lettuce, if using. Serve warm.

**Makes 4 servings**

> A little grated onion has a lot of moisture, so use it to keep your burgers juicy.

# Classic Cheeseburgers with Barbecue Spices

**Prep time: 10 minutes**
**Grilling time: 8 to 10 minutes**

1½  pounds ground chuck (80% lean)

**Rub**
1 teaspoon kosher salt
½ teaspoon pure chile powder
½ teaspoon light brown sugar
½ teaspoon granulated garlic
½ teaspoon paprika
¼ teaspoon celery seed
¼ teaspoon ground cumin
⅛ teaspoon freshly ground black pepper

4 thin slices Monterey Jack cheese
4 hamburger buns
  Ketchup, optional
  Mustard, optional

**1.** In a large bowl gently mix the ground chuck with the rub ingredients, incorporating the spices evenly. Gently shape into 4 patties of equal size and thickness, each about ¾ inch thick. With your fingertips or thumb, make a shallow depression about 1 inch wide in the center of each patty so the centers are about ½ inch thick (see page 89). This will help the patties cook evenly and prevent them from puffing on the grill.

**2.** Prepare a two-zone fire for high heat (see pages 14-15).

**3.** Brush the cooking grate clean. Grill the patties over *direct high heat*, with the lid closed as much as possible, until cooked to medium, 8 to 10 minutes, turning once when the patties release easily from the grate without sticking, and swapping their positions as needed for even cooking. Move the patties over indirect heat and place a slice of cheese on each to melt. With the lid open, grill the buns, cut sides down, over direct heat until toasted, 20 to 30 seconds. Place the cheeseburgers on the buns and add ketchup and mustard, if desired. Serve warm.

**Makes 4 servings**

# New England-Style Hot Dogs with Creamy Coleslaw

**Prep time: 10 minutes**
**Grilling time: 4 to 6 minutes**

**Coleslaw**
¼ small head green cabbage
⅓ cup mayonnaise
2 tablespoons sweet pickle relish
1 tablespoon cider vinegar
½ teaspoon celery seed
¼ teaspoon kosher salt
¼ teaspoon freshly ground black pepper

8 beef hot dogs
8 hot dog buns
  Ketchup, optional
  Mustard, optional

**1.** Remove and discard the core from the cabbage. Thinly slice or shred the cabbage, then chop it into ½-inch pieces. Put the cabbage in a medium bowl. In a small bowl mix the mayonnaise, relish, vinegar, celery seed, salt, and pepper. Add the mayonnaise mixture to the cabbage and mix well. Cover and refrigerate until ready to use. If desired, to fully incorporate the flavors, refrigerate for 1 hour or as long as 24 hours.

**2.** Prepare a two-zone fire for medium heat (see pages 14-15).

**3.** Brush the cooking grate clean. Grill the hot dogs over *direct medium heat*, with the lid open, until browned, 4 to 6 minutes, turning once and swapping their positions as needed for even cooking. During the last 30 seconds of grilling time, grill the buns over direct heat, cut sides down, until toasted. Place a grilled hot dog in each bun. Top with some coleslaw. Add ketchup and mustard, if desired. Serve warm.

**Makes 8 servings**

Classic Cheeseburgers with Barbecue Spices

New England-Style Hot Dogs with Creamy Coleslaw

# THE DUELING BUBBAS

Don Grissom and Derek Muller combine efforts in the uncle-and-nephew barbecue team called The Dueling Bubbas. Together these two have won more sanctioned tri-tip competitions than any other team in the world. Don says that the main reason for their success is they cook tri-tip like a brisket, smoking it over very low heat until extremely tender. Most others cook it like a steak, grilling it over hot coals and serving it medium rare (tasty but tough).

Another big difference is in their smoke. They use a specific combination of oak, hickory, and cherry. And they never use wood with the bark still attached. The Dueling Bubbas believe that bark gives off bitter, acrid aromas, so they examine wood chunks carefully before adding them to the coals.

The Dueling Bubbas put a high priority on knowing the ambient temperature right next to the tri-tip. Ideally it should be 240°F, they say, and one way to be sure is to slide the probe of a meat thermometer (connected wirelessly to a remote beeper) through a potato. While the potato sits on the cooking grate, along with the tri-tip, the thermometer lets you know when it's time to adjust the bottom vents.

# The Dueling Bubbas' Grand Tri-Tip

**Prep time: 15 minutes**
**Grilling time: 3 to 4 hours**

### Rub

- 2 teaspoons kosher salt
- 1 teaspoon pure chile powder
- 1 teaspoon granulated garlic
- 1 teaspoon sweet paprika
- ½ teaspoon ground coriander
- ½ teaspoon ground cumin
- ½ teaspoon freshly ground black pepper

<br>

- 1 tri-tip roast, 2½ to 3 pounds and about 1½ inches thick, trimmed of surface fat
- 2 tablespoons yellow mustard
- ¼ cup bottled barbecue sauce
- 2 tablespoons apple juice

<br>

- 7 fist-size dry wood chunks, 4 oak, 2 hickory, 1 cherry (not soaked)

**1.** Arrange 1 chimney starter of ashed-over charcoal briquettes in the bottom ring of a Weber® Smokey Mountain Cooker™ smoker (see pages 24-25). Immediately add about ½ chimney starter of unlit charcoal briquettes to the lit charcoal and use tongs to spread them out evenly. Leave all the bottom vents open. Put the middle section of the smoker, including the water pan, in place. Fill the water pan about three-quarters full with warm water. Put the cooking grates in place and close the lid. Be sure the top vent is open.

**2.** Carefully open the side door and lay the wood chunks on top of the charcoal. Close the side door. Initially the smoke coming out of the top vent will be harsh. Wait until the smoke turns much milder, 30 to 45 minutes.

**3.** In a small bowl mix the rub ingredients.

**4.** Cut an uncooked potato in half. Slide a meat thermometer (with wireless remote) through one of the halves, running parallel with the cut side. Make sure the sensor is exposed on one side of the potato. Wipe the sensor clean (see photo at left).

**5.** Remove the cold tri-tip from the refrigerator, lightly coat it with mustard, and season evenly with the rub.

Brush the top cooking grate clean. Place the tri-tip on the top cooking grate of the smoker. Place the potato, cut side down, next to the tri-tip. Close the lid.

**6.** Adjust the bottom vents so that the ambient temperature next to the tri-tip is about 240°F. Open the vents slightly to raise the temperature. Close the vents slightly to lower the temperature.

**7.** Cook and smoke the tri-tip until the internal temperature reaches 160°F, about 2 hours. At this point, stack two 16-inch squares of aluminum foil on a work surface. In a small bowl mix the barbecue sauce and apple juice. Place the tri-tip in the center of the top sheet of foil. Slather the barbecue sauce mixture all over the tri-tip. Fold up the ends of the foil and tightly wrap the tri-tip. Return the tri-tip to the smoker. Be sure the water pan is filled at least halfway with warm water.

**8.** Continue to cook the tri-tip until it is tender. When it is done and you stick an instant-read thermometer into the center (right through the foil), it will feel like you are sticking the thermometer into a ripe pear. Sometimes this tenderness happens when the internal temperature of the meat reaches 180°F, sometimes at 200°F. It might take 1 hour from the time you wrap the tri-tip. It might take 2 hours. Don't judge the doneness by the internal temperature or cooking time. Judge it by tenderness.

**9.** When fully cooked, remove the tri-tip from the smoker and let it rest for 10 to 20 minutes. Carefully unwrap the tri-tip, reserving the liquid, which can be served as a sauce. Pour the sauce into a serving bowl. Thinly slice the tri-tip across the grain. Serve warm with the sauce.

**Makes 6 servings**

# Tri-Tip with Avocado Sauce

**Prep time: 20 minutes**
**Grilling time: 30 to 45 minutes**

**Paste**
    1  tablespoon whole grain mustard
    1  tablespoon extra virgin olive oil
    1  tablespoon freshly ground black pepper
    2  teaspoons Worcestershire sauce
    1  teaspoon kosher salt

    1  tri-tip roast, 2 to 2½ pounds and
       about 1½ inches thick, trimmed of surface fat

**Sauce**
    1  ripe Haas avocado
    1  four-inch section English cucumber (seedless)
    ¼  cup sour cream
       Juice of 1 lime
    1  small garlic clove
    ½  teaspoon Worcestershire sauce
    ½  teaspoon Tabasco® sauce
    ½  teaspoon kosher salt
    ¼  teaspoon freshly ground black pepper

**1.** In a medium bowl mix the paste ingredients until smooth. Coat the tri-tip evenly with the paste. Let the tri-tip sit at room temperature for 20 to 30 minutes before grilling.

**2.** Scoop out the flesh of the avocado and combine it with the remaining sauce ingredients in a food processor. Process until smooth. The sauce should be fairly thick.

**3.** Prepare a two-zone fire for medium heat (see pages 14-15).

**4.** Brush the cooking grate clean. Grill the tri-tip over *direct medium heat*, with the lid closed as much as possible, until lightly charred on both sides, 10 to 15 minutes, turning and rotating as needed for even cooking. Move the tri-tip over *indirect medium heat* and cook to your desired doneness, 20 to 30 minutes for medium rare, turning and rotating as needed for even cooking. Remove from the grill and let rest for 10 minutes. Cut the tri-tip across the grain into very thin slices. Serve warm with the sauce on the side.

**Makes 6 to 8 servings**

# Smoke-Roasted Rack of Lamb with Anise-Garlic Paste

**Prep time: 10 minutes**
**Grilling time: 14 to 21 minutes**

**Paste**
3 tablespoons extra virgin olive oil
2 tablespoons ground anise seed
1 tablespoon minced garlic
1 tablespoon anise-flavored liqueur
2 teaspoons kosher salt
2 teaspoons freshly ground black pepper

2 racks of lamb, 1 to 1½ pounds each, frenched
1 large handful hickory or oak wood chips,
   soaked in water for at least 30 minutes

**1.** In a small bowl mix the paste ingredients.

**2.** Cut 3 or 4 slashes about ½ inch deep in the fat on top of each rack of lamb. Rub the paste all over the meat, making sure to get some in the cuts on top. Let the meat sit at room temperature for about 30 minutes before grilling. Wrap aluminum foil around the exposed bones to prevent them from charring.

**3.** Prepare a two-zone fire for medium heat (see pages 14-15).

**4.** Drain the wood chips and scatter them over the charcoal. Brush the cooking grate clean. When the chips begin to smoke, sear the racks, fat side down first, over *direct medium heat*, with the lid closed as much as possible, until golden brown all over, 4 to 6 minutes, turning once and swapping their positions as needed for even cooking. If flare-ups occur, move the racks over indirect heat until the flames die down.

**5.** When the racks are golden brown all over, move them, bone side down, over *indirect medium heat*, and continue to grill, with the lid closed as much as possible, to your desired doneness, 10 to 15 minutes for medium rare, rotating them as needed for even cooking.

**6.** Remove the racks from the grill, loosely cover with foil, and let rest for 5 minutes. Cut between the bones and serve warm.

**Makes 4 servings**

# Lamb Leg Steaks with Toasted Fennel and Green Olives

**Prep time: 20 minutes**
**Grilling time: 8 to 10 minutes**

**Rub**
1½ teaspoons fennel seed
  2 teaspoons finely chopped fresh fennel fronds
  2 teaspoons kosher salt
  1 teaspoon minced garlic
  ½ teaspoon freshly ground black pepper

  ¾ cup pitted, chopped Spanish green olives,
      about 5 ounces
  ¼ cup ¼-inch-diced roasted red bell pepper
  ½ cup ¼-inch-diced fennel bulb
3½ tablespoons extra virgin olive oil, divided
  3 teaspoons red wine vinegar, divided
      Kosher salt
      Freshly ground black pepper
  2 lamb leg steaks, each about 1 pound and 1 inch thick
  1 lemon, cut crosswise into ⅓-inch slices and seeded
  2 tablespoons finely chopped fresh Italian parsley

**1.** In a small skillet over medium heat, toast the fennel seed until fragrant, 2 to 4 minutes, shaking the skillet once or twice. Do not let them smoke. Grind them in a clean coffee mill or spice grinder. Reserve ½ teaspoon of the ground fennel for the olives. In a small bowl mix the rest of the ground fennel with the remaining rub ingredients.

**2.** In a medium bowl mix the olives with the bell pepper, fennel, 2 tablespoons of the oil, 2 teaspoons of the vinegar, and the reserved ground fennel seed. Add salt and pepper to taste.

**3.** Prepare a two-zone fire for high heat (see pages 14-15).

**4.** Rub both sides of the lamb with the remaining 1 teaspoon vinegar. Coat the lamb with 1 tablespoon of the oil. Season them evenly with the rub. Coat the lemon slices with the remaining ½ tablespoon of oil.

**5.** Brush the cooking grate clean. Grill the lamb over **direct high heat**, with the lid closed as much as possible, until cooked to your desired doneness, 8 to 10 minutes for medium rare, turning once and swapping their positions as needed for even cooking. During the last 2 minutes of grilling time, grill the lemon slices, one side only, over **direct high heat**, until slightly charred and softened. Remove the lamb and lemon slices from the grill. Let the lamb rest for 3 to 5 minutes before slicing. Mix the parsley with the olive mixture and spoon over the steaks. Garnish with the grilled lemons.

**Makes 4 servings**

The wispy green fronds, pale green bulb, and tender stalks of fennel are edible, but discard the tough, triangular core.

# Lamb Chops with Mustard Glaze and Toasted Pine Nuts

**Prep time: 20 minutes**
**Grilling time: 8 to 10 minutes**

**Glaze**
¼  cup Dijon mustard
¼  cup extra virgin olive oil
¼  cup grated Parmigiano-Reggiano cheese
½  teaspoon kosher salt
¼  teaspoon freshly ground black pepper

4  loin lamb chops, each about 4 ounces and
   1½ inches thick, trimmed of excess fat
½  cup pine nuts
2  tablespoons finely chopped fresh Italian parsley
2  tablespoons grated Parmigiano-Reggiano cheese

1. In a medium bowl mix the glaze ingredients.

2. Brush the lamb chops on both sides with the glaze. Let sit at room temperature for 20 to 30 minutes before grilling.

3. In a medium skillet over medium heat, toast the pine nuts until golden brown, 5 to 7 minutes, stirring occasionally. Transfer the nuts to a cutting board and roughly chop them. In a small bowl mix the nuts with the parsley and cheese.

4. Prepare a two-zone fire for high heat (see pages 14-15).

5. Brush the cooking grate clean. Grill the lamb chops over **_direct medium heat_**, with the lid closed as much as possible, until lightly charred on the surface and cooked to your desired doneness, 8 to 10 minutes for medium rare, turning once or twice and swapping their positions as needed for even cooking. If flare-ups occur, move the lamb chops temporarily over indirect heat. Serve warm with the nut mixture scattered over the top.

**Makes 4 servings**

# Cumin-Mint Leg of Lamb

**Prep time: 20 minutes**
**Marinating time: 1 to 2 hours**
**Grilling time: 30 to 45 minutes**

### Paste
2 teaspoons whole cumin seed
1 teaspoon whole black peppercorns
3 large garlic cloves
1 teaspoon kosher salt
1 teaspoon dried oregano
½ teaspoon crushed red pepper flakes
2 tablespoons extra virgin olive oil
1 tablespoon fresh lemon juice

1 boneless leg of lamb, 2½ to 3 pounds
⅓ cup tightly packed fresh mint leaves

### Sauce
1 cup sour cream
¼ cup Dijon mustard
1 tablespoon finely chopped fresh mint
½ teaspoon kosher salt

**1.** Using a mortar and pestle, pound the cumin seed and peppercorns into tiny pieces. Add the garlic, salt, oregano, and red pepper flakes. Pound the seasonings into tiny pieces. Add the oil and lemon juice. Mix to create a paste.

**2.** Carefully remove any excess fat and sinew from both sides of the lamb. Place the lamb, cut side up, on a clean work surface. The meat needs to be fairly uniform, 1 to 1½ inches thick. If any sections are thicker, cut them off and cook them separately or make shallow cuts on the bias into the thicker section and spread or "butterfly" the meat into a thinner section (see page 241). Spread half of the paste evenly over the inside of the lamb and the other half on the outside of the lamb. Lay the mint leaves down the middle

Nothing beats a mortar and pestle for grinding garlic with salt and extracting garlic's potent juices.

of the inside. Tightly roll the lamb into a long cylinder. Using kitchen twine, tie the lamb at 1½-inch intervals. Trim off the loose ends of the twine. Cover with plastic wrap and refrigerate for 1 to 2 hours.

**3.** Prepare a two-zone fire for medium heat (see pages 14-15).

**4.** In a small bowl whisk the sauce ingredients until smooth. Let the sauce and the lamb sit at room temperature for 20 to 30 minutes before grilling.

**5.** Brush the cooking grate clean. Grill the lamb, fat side down first, over **direct medium heat**, with the lid closed as much as possible, until golden brown all over, 10 to 15 minutes, turning once or twice and rotating as needed for even cooking. Move the lamb over **indirect medium heat** and cook to your desired doneness, 20 to 30 minutes for medium rare, rotating as needed for even cooking. Remove the lamb from the grill and let rest for about 10 minutes. Remove the twine. Cut the lamb crosswise into ½-inch slices. Serve warm or at room temperature with the sauce.

**Makes 6 servings**

# CAPTAIN ERIC "DISCO" DOMINIJANNI

Eric Dominijanni is a Captain in the United States Marine Corps. He is as patriotic a soldier as you will ever find. To him, fellow Marines are like family. They deserve the best of what he can provide. In Iraq, during the initial march into Baghdad, this cooking-obsessed soldier brought along his espresso maker and he even made paella for his troops in the back of his Assault Amphibian vehicle. "I may have had to fight like a barbarian, but I didn't have to eat like one," he said.

For lamb burgers, Captain D, as he likes to be called, explains the role of his ingredients in military terms. "The lamb is the main effort. The cheese is supporting effort #1, and the mission of all the other spices and flavors is to make the lamb a success."

Burger success depends on the proper heat of the charcoal. If the temperature is too high, a thick burger will burn on the outside before the inside is done, so Captain D recommends medium heat. Even at that "safe" temperature, he suggests that if the burger is turning too dark too fast, slide it over indirect heat for the final few minutes of cooking.

LIVE FIRE WISDOM · WEBER'S CHARCOAL

# Captain D's Lamb Burgers

**Prep time: 15 minutes**
**Chilling time: 2 to 4 hours**
**Grilling time: 10 to 13 minutes**

**Burgers**
  2  pounds freshly ground lamb
  ⅓  cup minced red onions
  2  tablespoons extra virgin olive oil
  2  tablespoons fresh lemon juice
  2  tablespoons finely chopped fresh Italian parsley
  2  tablespoons finely chopped fresh oregano
  2  teaspoons minced garlic
1½  teaspoons kosher salt
  1  teaspoon dried rosemary, optional
  1  teaspoon dried basil, optional
  ½  teaspoon freshly ground black pepper
  ½  teaspoon ground cumin

  8  slices sourdough bread, each about ½ inch thick
     Extra virgin olive oil
  8  thin slices ripe tomato
1½  cups lightly packed baby spinach leaves
  ¾  cup crumbled blue or feta cheese

**1.** In a large bowl gently mix the burger ingredients until evenly distributed. Gently shape the meat into 4 patties of equal size and thickness, each about ½ pound and 1 inch thick. With your fingertips or thumb, make a shallow depression about 1 inch wide in the center of each patty so the centers are about ¾ inch thick (see page 89). This will help the patties cook evenly and prevent them from puffing on the grill. Cover and refrigerate for 2 to 4 hours.

**2.** Prepare a two-zone fire for medium heat (see pages 14-15).

**3.** Brush the cooking grate clean. Grill the patties over *direct medium heat*, with the lid closed as much as possible, until well browned on the first side, 4 to 5 minutes. Turn the patties over and continue to grill over *direct medium heat*, 6 to 8 minutes for medium doneness, swapping their positions as needed for even cooking.

**4.** While the burgers are finishing on the second side, lightly brush the bread slices with oil and toast them over *indirect medium heat*, 1 to 2 minutes, turning once and swapping their positions as needed for even cooking.

**5.** Serve the lamb burgers warm on the toasted bread with the tomato slices, spinach, and cheese.

**Makes 4 big servings**

# Lamb Shish Kabobs with Tomato Tzatziki

**Prep time: 25 minutes**
**Chilling time: 1 hour**
**Grilling time: 5 to 7 minutes**

### Lamb

| | |
|---|---|
| 1½ | pounds freshly ground lamb |
| ¼ | cup minced green onions |
| 2 | teaspoons red wine vinegar |
| 1 | teaspoon minced garlic |
| ¾ | teaspoon kosher salt |
| ½ | teaspoon freshly ground black pepper |
| ¼ | teaspoon ground cumin |
| ⅛ | teaspoon ground cinnamon, optional |

### Sauce

| | |
|---|---|
| 1 | cup plain whole milk yogurt, preferably the thick, Greek style |
| ½ | cup finely chopped ripe tomato |
| ¼ | cup shredded carrot |
| 2 | tablespoons finely chopped fresh Italian parsley |
| 2 | teaspoons extra virgin olive oil |
| ½ | teaspoon minced garlic |
| ¼ | teaspoon kosher salt |
| ⅛ | teaspoon freshly ground black pepper |

16 wooden skewers, soaked in water for at least 30 minutes
Extra virgin olive oil

**1.** In a medium bowl gently mix the lamb ingredients until evenly distributed. Gently shape the lamb mixture into little rolls, each about 3 inches long and 1 inch in diameter. Cover and refrigerate for at least 1 hour before grilling.

**2.** In a small bowl mix the sauce ingredients. Cover and refrigerate until ready to serve.

**3.** After chilling the lamb rolls for at least 1 hour, place 2 side by side. Push a skewer through the rolls about 1 inch from their ends. Repeat with another skewer parallel to the first one. Double skewer the remaining lamb rolls. Lightly brush them on all sides with oil.

**4.** Prepare a two-zone fire for high heat (see pages 14-15).

**5.** Brush the cooking grate clean. Grill the lamb kabobs over ***direct high heat***, with the lid closed as much as possible, until nicely browned all over but still slightly pink and juicy in the center, 5 to 7 minutes, turning 2 or 3 times and swapping their positions as needed for even cooking. If flare-ups occur, finish cooking the lamb rolls over indirect heat. Serve warm with the sauce.

**Makes 4 servings**

PORK

# Brats with Spicy Stewed Peppers

**Prep time: 10 minutes**
**Grilling time: 35 to 45 minutes**

1 large red bell pepper
1 large yellow bell pepper
1 medium jalapeño chile pepper
1 medium red onion
¼ cup unsalted butter
1 teaspoon fennel seed
½ teaspoon kosher salt
¼ teaspoon freshly ground black pepper
1 cup beer
2 tablespoons spicy brown mustard
5 fresh bratwurst, preferably Johnsonville®
5 large hot dog buns

**1.** Prepare a two-zone fire for medium heat (see pages 14-15).

**2.** Remove and discard the stems and seeds from the bell peppers and jalapeño pepper. Cut the bell peppers lengthwise into ⅓-inch strips. Finely chop the jalapeño pepper. Cut the onion in half through the stem and root ends. Cut each half crosswise into ¼-inch slices.

**3.** Brush the cooking grate clean. In a 9 x 13-inch, heavy-duty foil pan over *direct medium heat*, melt the butter. Add the peppers, onion, fennel seed, salt, and pepper. Mix well with tongs. Cook the vegetables in the pan over *direct medium heat*, with the lid closed as much as possible, until they are tender and golden brown in spots, 10 to 15 minutes, stirring occasionally. If the vegetables brown too quickly, slide the pan over indirect heat and cook them there, with the lid closed.

**4.** When the vegetables are tender, add the beer and mustard. Mix well with tongs. Slide the pan over indirect heat to keep warm.

**5.** Grill the bratwurst over *direct medium heat*, with the lid closed as much as possible, until lightly charred on all sides, about 15 minutes, turning them every few minutes and swapping their positions as needed for even cooking. Then move the bratwurst to the pan over indirect heat. Smother them with the peppers and onion, close the lid, and cook until the bratwurst are fully cooked, 10 to 15 minutes. If the pan is getting too dry, add a little more beer.

**6.** Serve the bratwurst warm in the buns with the spicy pepper mixture on top.

**Makes 5 servings**

# Dutch Oven Jambalaya

**Prep time: 25 minutes**
**Grilling time: about 30 minutes**

2 cups reduced-sodium chicken broth
1½ cups V8® vegetable juice
2 teaspoons paprika
1½ teaspoons kosher salt
1 teaspoon Tabasco® sauce
¼ teaspoon freshly ground black pepper
2 tablespoons vegetable oil
1 cup ½-inch-diced yellow onion
½ cup ½-inch-diced red bell pepper
½ cup ½-inch-diced celery
½ pound smoked linguica, peeled and
  cut into ½-inch dice
2 teaspoons minced garlic
1 bay leaf
1½ cups long grain rice
½ pound Black Forest or other smoky ham,
  cut into ½-inch dice
1 pound medium shrimp (31-35 count), peeled and
  deveined, with tails left on
2 tablespoons finely chopped fresh Italian parsley

**1.** Prepare a two-zone fire for medium heat (see pages 14-15).

**2.** In a small ovenproof saucepan combine the chicken broth, vegetable juice, paprika, salt, Tabasco®, and pepper. Cover and place the saucepan over *direct medium heat*. When the liquid comes to a boil, remove the saucepan from the grill and set aside.

**3.** Preheat a large Dutch oven or ovenproof casserole dish over *direct medium heat*, with the grill's lid open, for 5 minutes. When hot, add the oil, onion, bell pepper, and celery. Cook until the vegetables soften, 3 to 5 minutes, stirring often. Add the linguica, garlic, and bay leaf and cook for 2 to 3 minutes, stirring often. Stir in the rice and ham. Add the warm chicken broth mixture and stir. Slide the pot to the edge of the fire or to the part of the grill where the liquid will barely simmer (do not boil). Cover the pot and simmer the rice until it is cooked through but not mushy, about 18 minutes, stirring once or twice, making sure there is still some liquid left. If the mixture looks dry, add a little water. If the liquid is boiling, move the pot farther away from the fire and rotate it for even cooking. Add the shrimp and stir to combine with the rice. Cover the pot and cook until the shrimp are cooked but still tender, 3 to 5 minutes. Remove and discard the bay leaf. Season to taste (careful, it's hot!), adding more salt and Tabasco® if needed.

**4.** Remove the pot from the grill and set aside with the lid on for about 5 minutes. Stir in the parsley and serve warm.

**Makes 6 servings**

# BABY BACK RIBS 101

Just those three words—baby back ribs—are enough to make me hungry. Abundantly marbled ribs, fragrant with smoke and spice, gratify me so thoroughly that I will gladly spend an afternoon tending to the small bed of embers required to barbecue them. That cooking experience alone, especially when combined with a televised baseball game and cold beer, has its own rewards. The real kicker, though, is when you pull two ribs apart and the crisp, caramelized surface tears, revealing unctuously soft, tender meat and a harmony of slow-cooked flavors.

Sadly, many chain restaurants settle for a grossly different standard of baby back ribs, offering us a cheap, uninteresting commodity coated in sweet, artificial flavors. For this reason I'm afraid most people don't even know how truly good barbecued ribs can be. To know for sure, you could mosey down South and order a couple racks from an authentic barbecue joint, or you could make the ribs yourself. What follows here is a primer to get you started. It reflects techniques I've been honing for years, but that is not to say this is the only way to barbecue ribs. You see, barbecuing ribs is like swinging a baseball bat. Once you've learned the fundamentals, you've got to personalize your style so it fits you naturally. But first, here are the fundamentals…

## How to Prepare Ribs

1. Choose ribs with a generous amount of meat, ideally an inch or so thick.

2. Trim any meat or fat that dangles from the bone side.

3. Also trim any tough sinew, a.k.a. silverskin, on the meaty side.

4. Slide the tip of a meat thermometer under the membrane and over a bone.

5. Pick up the edge of the membrane with a paper towel and peel it off.

6. Season the ribs lightly on the bone side. Don't forget the edges!

7. Season the ribs more heavily on the meaty side.

8. Arrange the ribs in a rack, with all of them facing the same direction.

# How to Barbecue Ribs

Rib masters will debate until the end of time about their spice rubs and sauces, about when to start smoking their ribs and which woods to use, about whether or not to finish their ribs wrapped in foil, and their countless other "be-all and end-all" techniques. But on one thing almost everyone can agree: low and slow. The temperature must be low enough to tenderize the rib meat slowly. If the temperature gets too high and the meat cooks too fast, you will be chewing on something as dry and tough as the cover of this book. Maintain an even bank of coals to the side of the ribs and moderate its temperature (ideally, between 250°F and 300°F) by opening and closing the grill's top vent.

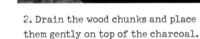

1. Begin cooking with the bone sides facing toward the charcoal.

2. Drain the wood chunks and place them gently on top of the charcoal.

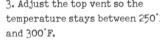

3. Adjust the top vent so the temperature stays between 250°F and 300°F.

4. About every hour, replenish the fire with 8 to 10 charcoal briquettes.

5. At the same time, gently sweep the ashes to keep the bottom vents clear.

6. Brushing with a mop sauce makes juicier, more flavorful ribs.

7. The ribs are done when the meat has shrunk back from most of the bones by ¼ inch or more. When you lift a rack by one end, it should bend and tear easily.

8. After brushing the ribs lightly with sauce, you may want to cook them for a few minutes longer, to crisp the surface. The total cooking time will be 3 to 4 hours.

# Classic Baby Back Ribs

**Prep time: 30 minutes**
**Grilling time: 3 to 4 hours**

**Rub**
- 2 tablespoons kosher salt
- 2 tablespoons paprika
- 4 teaspoons granulated garlic
- 4 teaspoons pure chile powder
- 2 teaspoons freshly ground black pepper
- 1 teaspoon ground cumin

- 4 racks baby back ribs, 2 to 2½ pounds each
- 4 medium chunks hickory wood, soaked in water for at least 30 minutes

**Barbecue sauce**
- ¾ cup apple juice
- ½ cup ketchup
- 3 tablespoons cider vinegar
- 2 teaspoons soy sauce
- 1 teaspoon Worcestershire sauce
- 1 teaspoon molasses
- ½ teaspoon pure chile powder
- ½ teaspoon granulated garlic
- ¼ teaspoon freshly ground black pepper

**Mop**
- 1 cup apple juice
- 3 tablespoons cider vinegar
- 2 tablespoons unsalted butter
- 2 tablespoons barbecue sauce (from above)

**1.** In a small bowl mix the rub ingredients.

**2.** Using a meat thermometer or dull knife, slide the tip under the membrane covering the back of each rack of ribs. Lift and loosen the membrane until it breaks, then grab a corner of it with a paper towel and pull it off. Season the ribs all over, putting more of the rub on the meaty sides than the bone sides. Do not press the spices into the surface of the meat. Arrange the ribs in a rib rack, with all the ribs facing the same direction (see page 114).

**3.** Prepare a two-zone fire for low heat (see pages 14-15), making sure the charcoal covers no more than one-third of the charcoal grate. Place a large, disposable drip pan on the empty side of the charcoal grate. Fill the pan about halfway with warm water.

**4.** Drain 2 chunks of hickory and place them on top of the charcoal. Put the cooking grate in place. Place the rib rack over *indirect low heat* (over the drip pan) as far from the charcoal as possible, with the bone sides facing toward the charcoal. Close the lid. Close the top vent about halfway. Let the ribs cook and smoke for 1 hour. During that time, maintain the temperature between 250°F and 300°F by opening and closing the top vent. Meanwhile, make the sauce and the mop.

**5.** In a small saucepan mix the barbecue sauce ingredients. Simmer for a few minutes over medium heat, and then remove the saucepan from the heat.

**6.** In another small saucepan mix the mop ingredients. Simmer for a few minutes over medium heat to melt the butter, and then remove the saucepan from the heat.

**7.** After the first hour of cooking, add 8 to 10 unlit charcoal briquettes and the remaining 2 hickory chunks (drained) to the fire. At the same time, lightly baste the ribs with some mop. Leaving the lid off for a few minutes while you baste the ribs will help the new briquettes to light. Close the lid and cook for another hour. During that time, maintain the temperature between 250°F and 300°F by opening and closing the top vent.

**8.** After 2 hours of cooking, add 8 to 10 unlit charcoal briquettes to the fire. Remove the ribs from the rib rack, spread them out on a clean work area and baste them thoroughly with some mop. Put them back in the rib rack, again all facing the same direction but this time turned over so that the ends facing down earlier now face up. Also position any ribs that appear to be cooking faster than the others toward the back of the rib rack, farther from the charcoal. Let the ribs cook for a third hour. During that time, maintain the temperature between 250°F and 300°F by opening and closing the top vent.

**9.** After 3 hours of cooking, check to see if any rack is ready to come off the grill. They are done when the meat has shrunk back from most of the bones by ¼ inch or more. When you lift a rack by picking up one end with tongs, the rack should bend in the middle and the meat should tear easily. If the meat does not tear easily, continue to cook the ribs. The total cooking time could be anywhere between 3 to 4 hours. Not all racks will cook in the same amount of time. Lightly brush the cooked ribs with some sauce and, if desired for crispiness, cook them over direct heat for a few minutes. Transfer to a baking sheet and tightly cover with aluminum foil. Let rest for 10 to 15 minutes before serving. Serve warm with the remaining sauce on the side.

**Makes 4 to 6 servings**

## PIT MASTER
# AMY ANDERSON

Initially Amy Anderson competed on the national barbecue circuit as a team of only one. She called herself Smokin' Bullet because her cooker of choice was "the bullet," otherwise known as the Weber® Smokey Mountain Cooker™ smoker. That was thirteen years ago. Since then she joined forces with her mother and changed the team name to Mad Momma & the Kids, winning the World Championship together in Ireland in 2000. Melanie Tapia came aboard next and helped the team win state championships in Washington, California, Arizona, and Idaho, always cooking on the bullet.

Amy and Melanie, now running their own restaurant, Ranch House BBQ, have some advice for anyone looking to make award-winning Pacific Northwest-style ribs: Add dried chunks of cherry and apple wood, along with a little mesquite, to the burning charcoal. It's a sweet, mild combination that complements the rub and sauce in this recipe.

## Ranch House BBQ Ribs

**Prep time: 30 minutes**
**Grilling time: 4 to 5 hours**

4  racks baby back ribs

**Rub**
2  tablespoons Lawry's® seasoned salt
1  tablespoon granulated sugar
1  tablespoon pure chile powder
1  tablespoon sweet paprika
1  teaspoon freshly ground black pepper
1  teaspoon garlic powder
1  teaspoon onion powder
1  teaspoon dry Italian seasoning

¼  cup yellow mustard

4  fist-size dry chunks apple/cherry/mesquite wood (not soaked)

**Sauce**
1  cup ketchup
⅓  cup cider vinegar
2  tablespoons light brown sugar
4  teaspoons Worcestershire sauce
1  tablespoon honey
1  tablespoon molasses
½  teaspoon garlic powder

1. Prepare the smoker (see pages 24-25) by lighting 3 paraffin cubes inside the charcoal chamber. Pour in enough unlit charcoal briquettes to fill a chimney starter 1½ times and spread out the charcoal evenly. Open the bottom vents completely. Wait until the charcoal is covered with gray ash, about 20 minutes.

2. Using a meat thermometer or dull knife, slide the tip under the membrane covering the back of each rack of ribs. Lift and loosen the membrane until it breaks, then grab a corner with a paper towel and pull it off (see page 114).

3. In a medium bowl mix the rub ingredients. Lightly coat both sides of each rack with mustard. This will help the rub stick to the meat. Sprinkle the rub evenly all over the racks. Let the racks sit at room temperature for 30 to 40 minutes before cooking.

4. When the charcoal is covered with gray ash, put the

water pan in place and fill it about ¾ full with warm water. Put the 2 cooking grates in place. Put the lid on, open the top vent completely, and insert a thermometer into one of the openings in the top vent. The temperature will rise to 350°F and higher. When it does, close the bottom vents completely. The temperature will slowly fall between 225°F and 250°F. When it does, open the bottom vents about halfway. Add two of the wood chunks to the charcoal and immediately close the door to maintain the temperature.

**5.** Place the racks in the rib rack, then place the rib rack in the middle of the top cooking grate, bending the ends if necessary to fit them on the grate. Close the lid. Be sure the bottom vents are open at least halfway. Let your ribs smoke. Maintain a temperature between 225°F and 250°F until the meat shrinks back at least ½ inch from the ends of at least several bones, 3½ to 4 hours. After the second hour, add the remaining wood chunks. If the temperature runs too high, close the bottom vents a bit. If the temperature falls too low, open the vents. If the vents are already open all the way, add 8 to 10 charcoal briquettes to the lit charcoal. Don't add charcoal unless it is already covered in gray ash (light it in a chimney starter). Carefully add the hot charcoal through the door into the charcoal chamber using long-handled tongs.

**6.** While the racks are smoking, make the sauce. In a saucepan combine the sauce ingredients. Whisk until

smooth. Bring to a simmer over medium heat, stirring occasionally. Remove the saucepan from the heat.

**7.** After the meat has shrunk back from the ends of the bones in several places, it is time to brush them with some sauce. Remove the rib rack from the smoker and put the lid back on to maintain the temperature. Lay each rack of ribs on a large work surface and lightly brush them on both sides with sauce (see photo below). Then return the racks to the rib rack, arranging them upside down as compared to how they were cooking earlier. Return the rib rack to the smoker and let the racks cook until the meat is so tender that when you pull two adjacent bones apart the meat between them tears easily, 30 to 60 minutes. If desired, brush the ribs with a little more sauce. Serve warm.

**Makes 4 to 6 servings**

# Cherry-Smoked Vietnamese Spareribs

**Prep time: 25 minutes**
**Marinating time: overnight to 24 hours**
**Grilling time: 3 to 4 hours**

**Marinade**
¼ cup Vietnamese fish sauce (nuoc mam)
¼ cup fresh orange juice
¼ cup finely chopped fresh cilantro
3 tablespoons dark brown sugar
2 tablespoons soy sauce
1 tablespoon tamarind paste, optional
2 teaspoons grated lime zest
1 tablespoon fresh lime juice
1 tablespoon finely chopped garlic
1 tablespoon finely chopped fresh ginger

2 racks St. Louis-style spareribs, 2½ to 3 pounds each
4 small handfuls cherry wood chips,
   soaked in water for at least 30 minutes
⅓ cup roughly chopped fresh cilantro

**1.** In a small bowl mix the marinade ingredients.

**2.** Cut off and discard the flap of meat hanging off the bone of the spareribs. Using a meat thermometer or dull knife, slide the tip under the membrane covering the back of each rack. Lift and loosen the membrane until it breaks, then grab a corner of it with a paper towel and pull it off.

**3.** Place the spareribs in a jumbo, resealable plastic bag and pour in the marinade. Press the air out of the bag and seal tightly. Turn the bag several times to distribute the marinade. Refrigerate overnight or as long as 24 hours, turning occasionally.

**4.** Prepare a two-zone fire for low heat (see pages 14-15). Place a large, disposable drip pan on the empty side of the charcoal grate. Fill it about halfway with warm water.

**5.** Let the spareribs sit at room temperature for 20 to 30 minutes before grilling. Remove the ribs from the bag and pour the marinade into a small saucepan. Bring to a boil over high heat, and boil gently for 30 seconds. Remove from the heat and set aside to use as a basting sauce.

**6.** Drain about half of the wood chips and scatter them over the burning charcoal. Brush the cooking grate clean. When the chips begin to smoke, lay the spareribs, bone side down, over ***indirect low heat***, for 1 hour.

**7.** After 1 hour, add 8 to 10 unlit charcoal briquettes to the burning charcoal. Also drain the remaining chips and scatter them over the charcoal. Begin basting the spareribs with the reserved marinade every 30 minutes. With the lid closed, grill the spareribs until the meat is quite tender and has pulled back at least ¼ inch from the ends of most of the bones, swapping the positions of the racks as needed for even cooking. The total cooking time will be 3 to 4 hours. You will need to add 8 to 10 unlit charcoal briquettes to the lit charcoal every hour or so to maintain indirect low heat.

**8.** When fully cooked, remove the racks from the grill, cover them with foil, and let rest for 10 to 15 minutes. Garnish with the cilantro and cut into individual ribs.

**Makes 4 to 6 servings**

## How to Trim Spareribs for the St. Louis-Style Cut

1. The triangular "point" at one end of the spareribs has very little meat, so remove it.

2. Also cut off the tough "rib tips," which extend just below the horizontal line of fat. Some folks like to cook these separately.

3. Trim any large pockets of fat or sinew. Also remove the "skirt," which is the chewy flap of meat that hangs from the middle of the other side.

4. If necessary, to fit the ribs on a grill or smoker, cut each rack in half.

# DAVE BIONDI

Dave Biondi has retired to the tranquility of barbecue. After thirty years as a probation officer in some tough neighborhoods in and around Oakland, California, he decided it was time to chill out. He bought a little smoker for his backyard and taught himself how to cook some respectable spareribs. Then he happened to meet a like-minded barbecue lover, Ric Gilbert, who was winning trophies left and right in the world of competition cooking. Ric invited Dave to join his team and encouraged a full-blown obsession with the impossible dream of making perfect barbecue.

## Dave's Memphis Wet Ribs

**Prep time: 40 minutes**
**Marinating time: 3 to 6 hours**
**Grilling time: 5 to 6 hours**

3 racks St. Louis-style spareribs,
  3 to 3½ pounds each
1 cup apple juice
  Juice of 1 lemon

**Rub**
1 tablespoon light brown sugar
1 tablespoon kosher salt
1 tablespoon paprika
1 tablespoon pure chile power
½ tablespoon ground cumin
½ tablespoon granulated garlic
1 teaspoon dry mustard
¼ teaspoon ground cayenne pepper
¼ teaspoon freshly ground black pepper

3 fist-size dry chunks oak/apple wood (not soaked)

**Sauce**
2 cups ketchup
½ cup light brown sugar
¼ cup cider vinegar
2 tablespoons yellow mustard
2 teaspoons freshly ground black pepper
2 teaspoons kosher salt
1 teaspoon Worcestershire sauce
1 teaspoon granulated garlic
  Juice of ½ lemon

½ cup apple juice (in a spray bottle)

**1.** Cut off and discard the flap of meat hanging off the bone of the spareribs. Using the handle of a teaspoon or a screwdriver, slide the tip under the membrane covering the back of each rack. Lift and loosen the membrane until it breaks, then grab a corner of it with a paper towel and pull it off. Place the spareribs in a large roasting pan or rimmed baking sheet and pour in the apple juice and lemon juice. Turn the spareribs over a few times to coat them evenly. Cover and refrigerate for 1 to 2 hours.

**2.** In a medium bowl mix the rub ingredients.

**3.** Remove the spareribs from the refrigerator. Pour off and discard the apple juice and lemon juice. Season the

spareribs all over with the rub. Cover and refrigerate for 2 to 4 hours. Remove the spareribs from the refrigerator 1 hour before grilling.

**4.** Prepare a Weber® Smokey Mountain Cooker™ smoker for 225°F to 250°F (see pages 24-25). Add 3 chunks of oak/apple wood to the burning charcoal briquettes.

**5.** Brush the cooking grates clean. Put the spareribs in the smoker, bone sides facing down, dividing them so they fit in a single layer on the two cooking grates. Cook them until they are done. This should take 5 to 6 hours. The meat will pull away from the ends of the bones by at least ¼ inch (often as much as 1 inch on some bones), and the meat will tear when you lift the racks on one end with tongs. While they cook, make the sauce.

**6.** In a medium saucepan mix all of the sauce ingredients except the lemon juice. Place the saucepan over low heat and cook for about 20 minutes, stirring occasionally. Add the lemon juice and cook for 5 more minutes. Remove the saucepan from the heat.

**7.** After about 3 hours of cooking, begin lightly spraying the spareribs on the meaty sides with apple juice every 30 minutes or so. This will help them brown. If the ribs look like they are about to burn on either side, remove them from the grill (close the lid quickly to maintain the heat) and wrap them individually in aluminum foil. Then return

them to the smoker. About 30 minutes before the spareribs are finished cooking, lightly brush them on both sides with some sauce.

**8.** When the spareribs are fully cooked and sauced, move them to a cutting board and let them rest for a few minutes. Then cut them into individual ribs. Serve warm with the remaining sauce on the side.

**Makes 6 servings**

Dave developed this recipe after a culinary trip to the legendary barbecue restaurants of Memphis, Tennessee. There the ribs traditionally have been prepared "dry," that is, basted with a vinegar sauce and coated with a dry spice mix just before serving. However, Dave leans toward the growing preference in Memphis for "wet" ribs, that is, slathered with mildly sweet, tomato-based barbecue sauce. Of course, common to all great ribs is smoke. For that Dave recommends chunks of oak and apple wood smoldering over charcoal briquettes. Stay clear of hickory, he says. Its strong flavor threatens to overpower his beautifully balanced sauce.

# Cajun-Spiced Pork Tenderloin with Red Bean Salad

**Prep time: 30 minutes**
**Grilling time: 15 to 20 minutes**

**Salad**
2   slices thick-cut bacon, cut into ½-inch dice
2   tablespoons peanut or vegetable oil
½   cup ¼-inch-diced yellow onion
½   cup ¼-inch-diced celery
½   cup ¼-inch-diced red bell pepper
1   can (16 ounces) red beans, rinsed
1   can (16 ounces) pinto beans, rinsed
2   tablespoons Creole or Dijon mustard
2   tablespoons granulated sugar
1   tablespoon cider vinegar
½   teaspoon Tabasco® sauce
¼   teaspoon kosher salt
3   tablespoons finely chopped fresh Italian parsley

**Rub**
2   teaspoons finely chopped fresh thyme
1½  teaspoons kosher salt
1   teaspoon granulated garlic
1   teaspoon granulated onion
1   teaspoon paprika
1   teaspoon light brown sugar
¾   teaspoon freshly ground black pepper
¼   teaspoon ground cayenne pepper

2   pork tenderloins, about 1 pound each,
    trimmed of silverskin
2   tablespoons Creole or Dijon mustard
    Peanut or vegetable oil

**1.** In a 10-inch skillet over medium heat, cook the bacon with the oil for about 2 minutes, stirring occasionally. Add the onion and cook until it begins to turn translucent, 3 to 4 minutes, stirring occasionally. Add the celery and bell pepper and cook for an additional 2 to 3 minutes, stirring occasionally. Add the remaining salad ingredients, except the parsley, and mix well. Cook for about 5 minutes, stirring occasionally. Remove the skillet from the heat and let the salad cool to room temperature. Adjust the seasonings with salt, if needed. Garnish with the parsley just before serving.

**2.** In a small bowl mix the rub ingredients.

**3.** Coat the pork all over with the mustard. Season evenly with the rub, pressing the spices into the meat, and then lightly coat the tenderloins with oil. Let the pork sit at room temperature for 20 to 30 minutes before grilling.

**4.** Prepare a two-zone fire for medium heat (see pages 14-15).

**5.** Brush the cooking grate clean. Grill the pork over *direct medium heat*, with the lid closed as much as possible, until the outsides are evenly seared, the centers are barely pink, and the internal temperature reaches 150°F, 15 to 20 minutes, turning every 5 minutes or so and swapping their positions as needed for even cooking. Remove the pork from the grill and let rest for 3 to 5 minutes before slicing on the bias. Serve warm with the salad.

**Makes 6 servings**

## Preparing a Pork Tenderloin

1. The sinewy layer on the surface is called silverskin.

2. Slip the tip of a sharp, thin knife under one end of the silverskin.

3. Grab the loosened end with your fingertips. Then slide the knife away from you just underneath the silverskin, with the knife blade angled slightly upwards.

4. The "cleaned" tenderloins should have hardly any visible silverskin or surface fat.

# Pork Tenderloin with Hoisin Dipping Sauce

**Prep time: 20 minutes**
**Marinating time: 4 to 6 hours**
**Grilling time: 15 to 20 minutes**

**Marinade**
¼ cup soy sauce
¼ cup dry sherry or mirin (sweet rice wine)
¼ cup hoisin sauce
2 tablespoons dark brown sugar
1 tablespoon oyster sauce
1 tablespoon Dijon mustard
1 tablespoon minced garlic
1 tablespoon minced ginger
1 teaspoon Chinese five-spice powder

2 pork tenderloins, about 1 pound each,
  trimmed of silverskin

**Glaze**
¼ cup honey
2 tablespoons dark brown sugar

**Sauce**
½ cup reserved marinade
1 tablespoon rice vinegar
3 tablespoons finely chopped scallion
1 tablespoon hoisin sauce
2 teaspoons toasted sesame seeds
1 teaspoon dark sesame oil
  Soy sauce

**1.** In a small bowl whisk the marinade ingredients. Place the pork in a large, resealable plastic bag and pour in the marinade. Press the air out of the bag and seal tightly. Turn the bag several times to distribute the marinade, place the bag in a bowl, and refrigerate 4 to 6 hours, turning occasionally.

**2.** In a small ovenproof saucepan whisk the honey and brown sugar.

**3.** Remove the pork from the marinade, reserving ½ cup of the marinade and discarding the rest. Let the tenderloins sit at room temperature for 20 to 30 minutes before grilling.

**4.** Prepare a two-zone fire for medium heat (see pages 14-15). While the charcoal burns down, warm the glaze over indirect heat until fluid.

**5.** Brush the cooking grate clean. Grill the pork over *direct medium heat*, with the lid closed as much as possible, for about 10 minutes, turning and swapping their positions once. Brush on the glaze. Continue to cook over *direct medium heat* until the meat is barely pink in the center and the internal temperature reaches 150°F, 5 to 10 minutes, turning and brushing with the glaze occasionally and swapping their positions as needed for even cooking. If the glaze begins to burn, move the pork over indirect heat to finish cooking. Remove the pork from the grill, brush one more time with the glaze, loosely cover with foil, and let rest for about 5 minutes while you make the dipping sauce.

**6.** In a small saucepan mix the reserved marinade, rice vinegar, and ¼ cup water. Bring to a boil. Reduce the heat and simmer for 2 minutes. Remove the saucepan from the heat and stir in the remaining sauce ingredients. Taste and add a few drops of soy if the sauce needs more saltiness and intensity.

**7.** Slice the pork and serve warm with the dipping sauce.

**Makes 6 servings**

# Five-Spice Pork Medallions with Red Curry Sauce

**Prep time: 25 minutes**
**Brining time: 1 hour**
**Grilling time: 15 to 20 minutes**

½ cup kosher salt
¼ cup dark brown sugar
2 garlic cloves, roughly chopped
2 pork tenderloins, about 1 pound each, trimmed of silverskin

**Sauce**
1 tablespoon vegetable oil
1 tablespoon tomato paste
1 teaspoon minced garlic
½ teaspoon red curry paste
1½ cups stirred coconut milk
1 tablespoon fresh lime juice
1 teaspoon dark brown sugar
½ teaspoon ground turmeric
¼ teaspoon kosher salt
¼ teaspoon freshly ground black pepper
1 tablespoon finely chopped fresh basil or mint

**Rub**
1 tablespoon Chinese five-spice powder
½ teaspoon freshly ground black pepper
¼ teaspoon kosher salt

Vegetable oil

**1.** In a large bowl whisk the salt, sugar, and garlic with 1 quart of cold water until the salt and sugar are dissolved. Submerge the pork in the brine. Refrigerate for 1 hour.

**2.** In a medium saucepan over medium heat, warm the oil. Add the tomato paste, garlic, and curry paste, stirring immediately to break apart the pastes. After 1 minute, add the remaining sauce ingredients, except the basil, and stir. Bring to a simmer. Cook until the mixture reaches a cream sauce consistency, 5 to 10 minutes, stirring occasionally. Add the basil during the last minute.

**3.** In a small bowl combine the rub ingredients. Remove the pork from the bowl and discard the brine. Pat dry with paper towels, and lightly coat with oil. Season evenly with the rub, pressing the spices into the meat. Let sit at room temperature for 20 to 30 minutes before grilling.

**4.** Prepare a two-zone fire for medium heat (see pages 14-15). Brush the cooking grate clean. Grill the pork over *direct medium heat*, with the lid closed as much as possible, until the centers are barely pink and the internal temperature reaches 150°F, 15 to 20 minutes, turning every 5 minutes or so and swapping their positions as needed for even cooking. Let the pork rest for 3 to 5 minutes. Reheat the sauce over medium heat. Carve the pork crosswise into thick slices. Serve warm with the sauce.

**Makes 4 to 6 servings**

# Pork Medallions with Port and Dried Cherry Sauce

**Prep time: 30 minutes**
**Grilling time: 15 to 20 minutes**

¾ cup dried cherries, about 4 ounces
1 cup port wine
1½ cups reduced-sodium beef stock
1 three-inch sprig of rosemary
1 teaspoon cornstarch
  Kosher salt
  Freshly ground black pepper
⅛ teaspoon ground nutmeg
⅛ teaspoon ground cinnamon
⅛ teaspoon ground cloves
2 pork tenderloins, about 1 pound each, trimmed of silverskin
2 tablespoons extra virgin olive oil

**1.** In a small saucepan bring ¾ cup of water to a boil and then add the cherries. Remove the saucepan from the heat and let cool to rehydrate the cherries.

**2.** Pour the port into a medium saucepan. Over medium-high heat reduce the port to about ¼ cup. Add the stock and rosemary, adjust the heat to a simmer, and reduce the liquid until the volume is reduced by half, about 10 minutes.

**3.** Strain the water from the cherries and place them back into their saucepan. In a small bowl, mix the cornstarch with 2 tablespoons of the hot stock mixture, then whisk it back into the medium saucepan. Return the mixture to a gentle boil. Add salt and pepper to taste. When the sauce is thickened, strain it through a fine sieve into the pan with the cherries.

**4.** Prepare a two-zone fire for medium heat (see pages 14-15).

**5.** In a small bowl mix the nutmeg, cinnamon, cloves, 1½ teaspoons of salt, and ¼ teaspoon of pepper. Lightly coat the pork on all sides with oil and season evenly with the spices. Let the pork sit at room temperature for 20 to 30 minutes before grilling.

**6.** Brush the cooking grate clean. Grill the pork over ***direct medium heat***, with the lid closed as much as possible, until the outsides are evenly seared, the centers are barely pink, and the internal temperature reaches 150°F, 15 to 20 minutes, turning every 5 minutes or so and swapping their positions as needed for even cooking.

**7.** Remove the pork from the grill and let rest for 3 to 5 minutes before slicing. Reheat the sauce over medium heat. Carve each tenderloin crosswise into thick slices. Serve warm with the cherry sauce.

**Makes 4 servings**

# Grill-Roasted Pork Loin with Tomatillo Salsa

**Prep time: 30 minutes**
**Brining time: 6 to 8 hours**
**Grilling time: 40 to 50 minutes**

**Brine**
¼ cup kosher salt
2 tablespoons granulated sugar
1½ teaspoons ground chipotle chile powder
Zest of 1 lime

1 boneless pork loin, about 2½ pounds, trimmed of excess fat

**Salsa**
4 slices bacon
10 medium tomatillos, husked and rinsed
2 medium Anaheim chile peppers, roughly chopped
1 small yellow onion, roughly chopped
1 large garlic clove
1 cup loosely packed fresh basil leaves
1 tablespoon extra virgin olive oil
1 teaspoon fresh lime juice
1 teaspoon light brown sugar
½ teaspoon kosher salt
¼ teaspoon freshly ground black pepper

Extra virgin olive oil
1 teaspoon kosher salt
½ teaspoon freshly ground black pepper
½ teaspoon granulated garlic

**1.** In a large bowl whisk the brine ingredients with 1 quart of cold water until the salt and sugar are dissolved. Place the pork in a large, resealable plastic bag and pour in the brine. Press the air out of the bag and seal tightly. Place the bag in a bowl and refrigerate for 6 to 8 hours.

**2.** In a large skillet over medium-low heat, cook the bacon until crisp, 10 to 12 minutes, turning occasionally. Remove the bacon from the pan and drain on paper towels, but leave the melted bacon fat in the skillet. Add the tomatillos, chile peppers, onion, and garlic. Cover the skillet and cook over medium heat until the tomatillos begin to collapse and the chiles are tender, 10 to 15 minutes, stirring occasionally to prevent browning. Transfer the mixture to a food processor or blender. Add the remaining salsa ingredients. Process until smooth. Finely chop the drained bacon and mix into the salsa.

**3.** Remove the pork from the bag and discard the brine. Pat dry with paper towels. Lightly coat the pork with oil and season evenly with the salt, pepper, and granulated garlic. Let sit at room temperature for 20 to 30 minutes before grilling.

**4.** Prepare a two-zone fire for medium heat (see pages 14-15).

**5.** Brush the cooking grate clean. Grill the pork over ***direct medium heat***, with the lid closed as much as possible, until the surface is dark brown and the internal temperature reaches 150°F, 40 to 50 minutes, turning and rotating every 10 minutes for even cooking. If the pork begins to burn, finish cooking it over indirect heat, turning occasionally (total cooking time will be slightly longer). Remove the pork from the grill and let rest at room temperature for about 5 minutes. Meanwhile, reheat the salsa over medium heat. Cut the pork crosswise into slices about ½ inch thick and serve warm with the salsa.

**Makes 6 to 8 servings**

# Pork T-Bone Steaks with Whiskey Barbecue Sauce

**Prep time: 10 minutes**
**Grilling time: 8 to 12 minutes**

**Rub**
 2 teaspoons paprika
 1 teaspoon light brown sugar
 1 teaspoon kosher salt
 ½ teaspoon freshly ground black pepper
 ½ teaspoon granulated garlic
 ½ teaspoon granulated onion
 ¼ teaspoon ground cumin
 ⅛ teaspoon ground cloves
   Pinch ground cayenne pepper

**Sauce**
 ⅓ cup bottled steak sauce
 ⅓ cup ketchup
 ¼ cup aged Scotch whiskey
 2 tablespoons Dijon mustard
 2 tablespoons light brown sugar
 ½ teaspoon granulated onion

   Kosher salt
   Freshly ground black pepper

 4 pork T-bone steaks, 10 to 12 ounces each
   and about 1¼ inches thick
   Peanut oil
 1 large handful hickory chips, soaked in water
   for at least 30 minutes

**1.** In a small bowl mix the rub ingredients.

**2.** In a small, heavy-bottom saucepan whisk the sauce ingredients. Bring to a boil over high heat, reduce the heat, and simmer over very low heat for 20 minutes, stirring frequently. Season to taste with salt and pepper.

**3.** Lightly coat the steaks on both sides with oil. Season with the rub, pressing the spices into the meat. Let the steaks sit at room temperature for 20 to 30 minutes before grilling.

**4.** Prepare a two-zone fire for high heat (see pages 14-15).

**5.** Drain the hickory chips and scatter them over the charcoal. Brush the cooking grate clean. Sear the steaks over ***direct high heat***, with the lid closed as much as possible, until well marked, 6 to 8 minutes, turning once and swapping their positions as needed for even cooking. Then move the steaks over ***indirect high heat*** and continue grilling, with the lid closed, until the meat is pink and juicy, 2 to 4 minutes. Remove from the grill and let rest for 3 to 5 minutes. Warm the sauce over direct heat. Serve the steaks warm with the sauce on the side.

**Makes 4 servings**

# Orange-Ginger Pork Chops

**Prep time: 10 minutes**
**Marinating time: 1 to 2 hours**
**Grilling time: 6 to 10 minutes**

### Marinade
- 1 cup fresh orange juice
- 2 teaspoons grated fresh ginger
- 1 teaspoon minced garlic
- 1 teaspoon dark sesame oil
- ½ teaspoon kosher salt
- ¼ teaspoon crushed red pepper flakes

- 4 bone-in pork rib chops, each about ¾ inch thick
  Vegetable oil
- ½ teaspoon kosher salt
- ¼ teaspoon freshly ground black pepper

**1.** In a medium bowl mix the marinade ingredients.

**2.** Place the pork chops in a large, resealable plastic bag and pour in the marinade. Press the air out of the bag and seal tightly. Turn the bag several times to distribute the marinade, place the bag flat in a rimmed pan, and refrigerate for 1 to 2 hours, turning occasionally.

**3.** Prepare a two-zone fire for high heat (see pages 14-15).

**4.** Remove the pork chops from the bag and reserve the marinade. Pat the chops dry on both sides with paper towels and brush off the bits of ginger and garlic. Lightly coat the chops on both sides with oil. Season evenly with the salt and pepper. Let sit at room temperature for 20 to 30 minutes before grilling. Meanwhile, pour the marinade into a small saucepan, bring to a boil over high heat, and boil for 30 seconds. Remove the saucepan from the heat.

**5.** Brush the cooking grate clean. Grill the pork chops over **_direct high heat_**, with the lid closed as much as possible, until the surface is well marked but not burnt, 3 to 5 minutes, turning once or twice and swapping their positions as needed for even cooking. Move the chops over **_indirect high heat_** and cook until firm to the touch but still slightly pink in the center, 3 to 5 minutes, turning once or twice and swapping their positions as needed for even cooking. Baste the chops occasionally with the boiled marinade. Remove from the grill. Serve warm.

**Makes 4 servings**

# Brined Pork Chops with Sweet Papaya Relish

**Prep time: 20 minutes**
**Brining time: 2 hours**
**Grilling time: 10 to 15 minutes**

**Brine**
⅓  cup granulated sugar
⅓  cup kosher salt

6  boneless, center cut pork chops, about 6 ounces each
   and 1¼ inches thick

**Relish**
⅓  cup granulated sugar
¼  cup rice vinegar
¼  cup thinly sliced scallions, white and light green parts
2  tablespoons fresh lime juice
1  teaspoon minced jalapeño chile pepper
½  teaspoon ground cumin
½  teaspoon kosher salt
⅛  teaspoon freshly ground black pepper
4  cups ½-inch-diced ripe papaya, about 2 pounds
¾  cup ¼-inch-diced red bell pepper
¼  cup finely chopped fresh basil

   Vegetable oil
1  teaspoon kosher salt
¾  teaspoon freshly ground black pepper

**1.** In a large bowl whisk the sugar and salt with 6 cups of cold water until the sugar and salt are dissolved. Submerge the pork chops in the brine. Cover the bowl and refrigerate for 2 hours.

**2.** In a large saucepan combine the sugar, vinegar, scallions, lime juice, jalapeño, cumin, salt, and pepper. Bring to a boil, and then add the papaya and bell pepper. Mix well. Simmer over medium heat until the papaya is very soft but not mushy, about 5 minutes, stirring occasionally. Let cool to room temperature. Add the basil, and adjust the seasonings, if necessary. Let sit at room temperature while you grill the chops.

**3.** Prepare a two-zone fire for medium heat (see pages 14-15).

**4.** Take the chops out of the bowl and discard the brine. Dry both sides with paper towels. Lightly coat them on both sides with oil. Season evenly with the salt and pepper.

**5.** Brush the cooking grate clean. Grill the chops over ***direct medium heat***, with the lid closed as much as possible, until barely pink in the center or until the internal temperature reaches 150˚F, 10 to 15 minutes, turning once and swapping their positions as needed for even cooking. Serve warm with the relish.

**Makes 6 servings**

# Pork and Mango Kabobs

**Prep time: 20 minutes**
**Grilling time: 6 to 8 minutes**

    1  cup fresh orange juice
    2  tablespoons honey
       Finely grated zest of 1 lime
    2  tablespoons fresh lime juice
    ½  teaspoon finely grated fresh ginger
    ¼  teaspoon kosher salt
    1  tablespoon thinly sliced fresh mint (chiffonade)
    2  pounds boneless pork loin chops, trimmed of excess
       fat and cut into 1- to 1½-inch cubes
    2  tablespoons extra virgin olive oil
    1  teaspoon pure chile powder
    1  teaspoon kosher salt
    ½  teaspoon ground cumin
    ½  teaspoon granulated garlic
    ½  teaspoon dried oregano
    ¼  teaspoon freshly ground black pepper
    2  large mangoes, 12 to 16 ounces each, peeled and cut
       into ½- to 1-inch chunks
   16  wooden skewers, soaked in water for
       at least 30 minutes

**1.** In a small saucepan combine the orange juice, honey, lime zest, lime juice, ginger, and salt. Bring the mixture to a simmer over medium heat. Simmer gently until the mixture thickens to a syrupy consistency and ½ cup of the liquid remains, 20 to 30 minutes. Allow to cool. Add the mint.

**2.** Place the pork in a medium bowl. Add the oil and mix to coat evenly. In a small bowl mix the chile powder, salt, cumin, granulated garlic, oregano, and pepper. Sprinkle the mixture over the pork and mix to coat evenly.

**3.** Thread the pork cubes and mango chunks alternately onto skewers. Let the kabobs sit at room temperature for 20 to 30 minutes before grilling.

**4.** Prepare a two-zone fire for high heat (see pages 14-15).

**5.** Brush the cooking grate clean. Grill the kabobs over **direct high heat**, with the lid closed as much as possible, until the pork is barely pink in the center, 6 to 8 minutes, turning once and swapping their positions as needed for even cooking. Serve warm with the sauce drizzled on top.

**Makes 4 to 6 servings**

---

# Grilled Prosciutto and Provolone Panini

**Prep time: 10 minutes**
**Grilling time: 6 to 8 minutes**

    4  flat sandwich rolls
  2-3  tablespoons stone ground mustard
   12  pieces thinly sliced prosciutto, about ½ pound
    6  thin slices provolone cheese, about 6 ounces total
    2  roasted red bell peppers, cut into 1 inch strips
  2-3  cups loosely packed fresh basil leaves
       Olive oil

**1.** Prepare a two-zone fire for low heat (see pages 14-15).

**2.** Cut the rolls in half lengthwise. Spread an even layer of mustard on the cut side of each roll. Cut the slices of prosciutto into a few pieces and divide them evenly among the bottom halves of the rolls. Cut each slice of provolone in half and arrange those pieces over the prosciutto. Then arrange the peppers and basil leaves on top. Put the top halves of the rolls in place. Press down on each sandwich so it is compacted.

**3.** Lightly brush each roll on both sides with olive oil. Place the sandwiches on the grill with heavy weights (large enameled baking dishes, cast iron skillets, etc.) on top of the sandwiches. Grill over **direct low heat**, with the lid open, until the bread is toasted and the cheese is melted, 6 to 8 minutes, turning each sandwich once and swapping their positions as needed for even cooking.

To press each sandwich, place a heavy skillet on top, or top all the sandwiches with a baking sheet and weigh it down with bricks.

**4.** Transfer the sandwiches to a cutting board and cut in half, or into smaller pieces if serving as an appetizer. Serve warm.

**Makes 4 servings**

Pork and Mango Kabobs

Grilled Prosciutto and Provolone Panini

# Honey-Glazed Ham Steaks with Black-Eyed Peas

**Prep time: 15 minutes**
**Grilling time: 8 to 11 minutes**

**Salsa**
- 1 can (15 ounces) black-eyed peas or small white beans, rinsed
- 1 cup cored, seeded, finely diced ripe tomatoes
- ¼ cup thinly sliced scallions
- 2 tablespoons finely chopped fresh Italian parsley
- 2 tablespoons fresh lime juice
- 2 tablespoons extra virgin olive oil
- ½ teaspoon kosher salt
- ¼ teaspoon freshly ground black pepper

- 2 tablespoons extra virgin olive oil
- 1 tablespoon honey
- 1 tablespoon Dijon mustard
- ¼ teaspoon prepared chili powder
- 2 smoked, bone-in ham steaks, each about 1¼ pounds and ½ inch thick

**1.** In a medium bowl combine the salsa ingredients. Mix well. If desired, to fully incorporate the flavors, let the salsa sit at room temperature for 1 to 2 hours. Adjust the seasonings, if desired.

**2.** Prepare a two-zone fire for medium heat (see pages 14-15).

**3.** In a small bowl mix the oil, honey, mustard, and chile powder until you have a smooth glaze.

**4.** Brush the cooking grate clean. Grill the ham steaks over ***direct medium heat***, with the lid closed as much as possible, until lightly marked on both sides, 6 to 8 minutes, turning and rotating once or twice. Lightly glaze the steaks with the mustard mixture and continue to grill, with the lid closed as much as possible, until the edges turn crispy and the steaks are hot, 2 to 3 minutes longer, glazing, turning, and rotating once or twice.

**5.** Remove the steaks from the grill and cut into serving pieces. Serve warm with the salsa (leave most of the liquid released by the salsa ingredients in the bowl).

**Makes 4 servings**

# Barbecued Ham with Sticky Orange Glaze

**Prep time: 15 minutes**
**Grilling time: 1¼ to 2 hours**

1 bone-in, smoked ham (with no added water),
   8 to 10 pounds
2 large handfuls pecan or apple wood chips,
   soaked in water for at least 30 minutes

**Glaze**
¾ cup fresh orange juice
½ cup Heinz® chili sauce
⅓ cup cider vinegar
2 tablespoons brown sugar
1 tablespoon Dijon mustard
1 tablespoon soy sauce
½ teaspoon freshly ground black pepper

**1.** Let the ham sit at room temperature for about 1 hour before cooking.

**2.** Prepare a three-zone split fire for low heat (see page 17). Place a large, disposable drip pan between the two piles of charcoal and fill the pan halfway with warm water. Drain the wood chips and add them to the charcoal.

**3.** Place the ham, flat side down, in a 9 x 13-inch, heavy-duty foil pan. Place the pan on the cooking grate and pour about 1 cup of water in the pan. Close the lid and cook the ham over *indirect low heat* for 1 hour. Ideally, the temperature will be between 300°F and 350°F when the ham goes on the grill, and after 1 hour the temperature will hover around 300°F. If the temperature is running too high, close the top vent as much as halfway. If the temperature is falling too low, open the top vent all the way.

**4.** In a small saucepan combine the glaze ingredients and simmer until about 1 cup remains, 5 to 10 minutes, stirring occasionally.

**5.** After 1 hour, begin brushing the top surface of the ham (not the flat side) with the glaze. If the pan is nearly dry, add about ½ cup of water and continue to cook over *indirect low heat*. The water in the pan should barely simmer, so adjust the top vent accordingly. Replenish the charcoal as needed to maintain indirect low heat, adding 10 to 12 unlit charcoal briquettes to the lit charcoal every 45 minutes to 1 hour.

**6.** Continue to cook and glaze the ham until the internal temperature reaches 135°F. If the ham begins to look too dark, cover it with foil and stop glazing. The total cooking time will be 1¼ to 2 hours (roughly 10 minutes per pound).

**7.** Carefully remove the ham from the foil pan and transfer it to a cutting board. Tent the ham with foil and let rest for 15 to 20 minutes. Carve the ham and serve warm.

**Makes 10 to 12 servings**

# Carolina "Red" Pulled Pork Shoulder

**Prep time: 45 minutes**
**Grilling time: 5 to 7 hours**

### Rub

- 1  tablespoon kosher salt
- 1  tablespoon light brown sugar
- 2  teaspoons paprika
- 1  teaspoon prepared chili powder

- 1  boneless pork shoulder, 5 to 6 pounds, with a thin layer of exterior fat
- 2  large handfuls hickory wood chips, soaked in water for at least 30 minutes

### Sauce

- 1  cup apple cider vinegar
- 1  cup ketchup
- ¼  cup lightly packed light brown sugar
- 1  teaspoon Tabasco® sauce
- 1  teaspoon Worcestershire sauce
- 1  teaspoon kosher salt

- 12  hamburger buns

**1.** In a small bowl mix the rub ingredients.

**2.** Coat the pork shoulder all over with the rub and press the spices into the meat. Allow the pork to sit at room temperature for 30 to 40 minutes before grilling. If the pork does not hold together naturally in one piece, tie the pork with 3 or 4 lengths of kitchen twine, each about 3 feet long.

**3.** Prepare a two-zone fire for low heat (see pages 14-15). Place a large, disposable drip pan on the empty side of the charcoal grate and fill it about halfway with warm water. Drain the wood chips and scatter them across the charcoal.

**4.** Brush the cooking grate clean. Grill the pork, fat side up, over *indirect low heat*, with the lid closed as much as possible, for 5 to 7 hours, rotating the pork as needed for even cooking.

**5.** In a large heavy-bottom saucepan, whisk the sauce ingredients. Bring to a simmer over medium heat and cook for about 5 minutes, stirring occasionally. Taste and adjust the seasonings, if necessary. It should be spicy and tangy.

**6.** Cook the pork until the internal temperature at the center of the meat reaches 190°F. When it is done, the meat should be tender enough that you can easily tear it apart with two forks (see photo at right). Replenish the charcoal as needed to maintain indirect low heat, adding 10 to 12 unlit charcoal briquettes to the lit charcoal every 45 minutes to 1 hour. Again, the total cooking time should be 5 to 7 hours.

**7.** Transfer the pork to a baking sheet and tightly cover with aluminum foil. Let the pork rest for 30 minutes.

**8.** Pull the warm meat apart with your fingers or use two forks to shred the meat. Discard any large pieces of fat or sinew. In a large bowl moisten the pork with as much sauce as you like (you may not need all of it). Pile the pork on hamburger buns. Serve warm.

**Makes 10 to 12 servings**

Shred the meat with your fingers or two forks. Discard any clumps of fat, but keep bits of the "bark," which is the crusty outer layer fragrant with smoke and spice.

# Smoky Pork Chile Verde

**Prep time: 30 minutes**
**Grilling time: 2½ to 3½ hours**

**Rub**

- 1  tablespoon kosher salt
- 2  teaspoons pure chile powder
- 2  teaspoons dried oregano
- 1  teaspoon granulated garlic
- 1  teaspoon ground cumin

- 1  boneless pork shoulder, 4 to 4½ pounds, trimmed of excess surface fat
- 8  medium tomatillos, husked and rinsed
- 1  can (7 ounces) chopped green chiles with liquid
- 4  medium garlic cloves
- 1  small onion, roughly chopped
- 2  teaspoons dried oregano
- ¾  cup dark Mexican beer
- 2  handfuls hickory wood chips, soaked in water for at least 30 minutes
- ¼  cup finely chopped fresh cilantro
- 1  teaspoon Tabasco® chipotle pepper sauce
     Kosher salt
     Freshly ground black pepper
- 6  cups steamed white rice
- 1  cup sour cream
- 1  lime, cut into eighths

**1.** Prepare a three-zone split fire for low heat (see page 17). Carefully place a large, disposable drip pan between the piles of charcoal and fill it about halfway with warm water.

**2.** In a small bowl mix the rub ingredients. Coat the pork on all sides with the rub, massaging the spices into the meat. Let the pork sit at room temperature for 20 to 30 minutes before grilling.

**3.** In a food processor or blender, purée the tomatillos, canned chiles, garlic, onion, oregano, and beer.

**4.** Drain the hickory chips and scatter them over the two piles of charcoal. Brush the cooking grate clean. When the chips start to smoke, place the pork in the center of the cooking grate, close the lid, and smoke-roast the pork over **indirect low heat** for 30 minutes.

**5.** Remove the pork from the grill and immediately close the lid to maintain the temperature. Place the pork in a 9 x 13-inch, heavy-duty foil pan. Pour the tomatillo mixture around the pork so it comes up the sides of the pork by 1 inch or so. Tightly seal the pan with foil, and place the pan in the center of the cooking grate. Cook the pork over **indirect low heat**, with the lid closed as much as possible, until the internal temperature of the meat reaches 190°F and the meat is so tender that it tears easily with a fork, 2 to 3 hours, depending on how steady the temperature is. To maintain the temperature, add 5 or 6 charcoal briquettes to each pile of charcoal every hour or so from the time you began to smoke the pork.

**6.** When the pork is fully cooked, carefully remove the pan from the grill. Unwrap the pork (be careful of the steam) and transfer it to a cutting board. Chop the pork into ½-inch chunks and shreds, discarding any large pieces of fat or tough pieces of meat. Pour the pan liquid into a large saucepan and spoon off most of the surface fat. Add the shredded meat and simmer the mixture uncovered for a few minutes to blend the flavors. Season with the cilantro, Tabasco®, and salt and pepper to taste. The chile verde may be made up to this point 1 day ahead of serving and refrigerated overnight. Warm the chile verde over a slow simmer before serving.

**7.** Serve the chile verde warm in bowls with steamed rice. Pass the sour cream, lime wedges, and a bottle of Tabasco®.

**Makes 6 to 8 servings**

POULTRY

# Chicken Satay with Balinese Peanut Sauce

**Prep time: 30 minutes**
**Marinating time: 1 to 4 hours**
**Grilling time: 8 to 12 minutes**

### Marinade
- ¼ cup peanut oil
- Grated zest and juice of 1 lime
- 1 tablespoon fish sauce
- 2 teaspoons chile-garlic sauce, such as Sriracha
- 1 teaspoon ground coriander
- 1 teaspoon ground cumin

- 4 boneless, skinless chicken breast halves (without tenders), 8 to 10 ounces each

### Salad
- 1 eight-inch section English cucumber (seedless)
- 1 tablespoon minced fresh mint
- 2 teaspoons fresh lime juice
- 1 teaspoon granulated sugar
- ½ teaspoon kosher salt

### Sauce
- ½ cup smooth peanut butter
- ½ cup stirred coconut milk
- 2 tablespoons fresh lime juice
- 2 teaspoons chile-garlic sauce, such as Sriracha
- 2 teaspoons fish sauce

- 16 wooden skewers, soaked in water for at least 30 minutes

1. In a medium bowl mix the marinade ingredients.

2. Cut each chicken breast crosswise into ½-inch slices. Place the chicken slices in the bowl with the marinade and mix to coat all the slices thoroughly. Cover and refrigerate for at least 1 hour and as long as 4 hours.

3. Quarter the cucumber lengthwise, and then cut the quarters crosswise as thinly as possible. In a medium bowl mix the cucumber slices with the remaining salad ingredients. Set aside at room temperature for at least 30 minutes.

4. In a small saucepan combine the sauce ingredients. Set the saucepan over very low heat and cook until the sauce is smooth, 3 to 5 minutes, whisking occasionally, but do not let the sauce simmer. If the sauce seems too thick, whisk in 1 to 2 tablespoons of water. Remove the saucepan from the heat.

5. Remove the chicken from the bowl and discard the marinade. Thread the chicken slices lengthwise on the skewers, 2 or 3 slices per skewer, keeping the skewers inside the meat as much as possible.

6. Prepare a two-zone fire for high heat (see pages 14-15).

7. Brush the cooking grate clean. Working in 2 batches, grill the chicken skewers over ***direct high heat***, with the bare wooden section of the skewers lying over indirect heat to keep them from burning. Close the lid and cook until the meat is firm to the touch and no longer pink in the center, 3 to 4 minutes on the first side and 1 to 2 minutes on the second side, turning once and swapping their positions as needed for even cooking. Meanwhile, reheat the sauce over very low heat. Serve the chicken warm with the salad and sauce.

**Makes 4 servings**

# Mojo-Marinated Chicken Tacos with Tomatillo Salsa

**Prep time: 25 minutes**
**Marinating time: 2 hours**
**Grilling time: 16 to 20 minutes**

**Marinade**
¼ cup fresh orange juice
3 tablespoons fresh lime juice
3 tablespoons extra virgin olive oil
2 tablespoons finely chopped fresh cilantro
1 tablespoon finely chopped jalapeño chile pepper, including seeds
1 tablespoon minced garlic
¾ teaspoon ground cumin
½ teaspoon kosher salt

4 boneless, skinless chicken breast halves (without tenders), about 8 ounces each

**Salsa**
1 medium yellow onion, cut into ½-inch slices
Extra virgin olive oil
10 medium tomatillos, about ½ pound total, husked and rinsed
1 small jalapeño chile pepper, stem removed
¼ cup lightly packed fresh cilantro leaves and tender stems
1 medium garlic clove
½ teaspoon dark brown sugar
½ teaspoon kosher salt

12 flour tortillas (8 inches)
¾ cup sour cream

**1.** In a medium bowl whisk the marinade ingredients. Place the chicken in a large, resealable plastic bag and pour in the marinade. Press out the air and seal the bag tightly. Turn the bag to distribute the marinade, place the bag in a bowl, and refrigerate for 2 hours.

**2.** Prepare a two-zone fire for high heat (see pages 14-15).

**3.** Lightly brush the onion slices on both sides with oil. Brush the cooking grate clean. Grill the onion slices,

Pick tomatillos that are nice and firm.

tomatillos, and jalapeño over ***direct high heat***, with the lid closed as much as possible, until lightly charred, 6 to 8 minutes, turning once or twice and swapping their positions as needed for even cooking. Be sure the tomatillos are completely soft as you remove them from the grill. Combine the onion slices, tomatillos, and jalapeño in a food processor along with the remaining salsa ingredients. Process until fairly smooth. Taste and adjust the seasonings. Pour the salsa into a serving bowl.

**4.** Check the heat of the grill. You may need to add more charcoal to the fire for medium heat. Remove the chicken from the bag and discard the marinade. Separate the tortillas into 2 piles of 6 tortillas each. Wrap each pile in a sheet of aluminum foil. When the fire is ready, brush the cooking grate clean. Grill the chicken over ***direct medium heat***, with the lid closed as much as possible, until the meat is firm to the touch and completely opaque in the center, 10 to 12 minutes, turning once or twice and swapping their positions as needed for even cooking. At the same time, grill each packet of tortillas over ***indirect medium heat*** until warm and soft, 3 to 5 minutes. Remove the chicken and tortillas from the grill. Keep the tortillas in the foil while you slice the chicken as thinly as possible.

**5.** Put some sliced chicken in each warm tortilla. Pass the salsa and sour cream for toppings. Serve right away.

**Makes 4 to 6 servings**

# Spike's Baja Burritos

**Prep time: 30 minutes**
**Grilling time: 10 to 14 minutes**

4   boneless, skinless chicken breast halves,
     6 to 8 ounces each
     Extra virgin olive oil
½   teaspoon ground cumin
½   teaspoon kosher salt
¼   teaspoon freshly ground black pepper
2   medium poblano chile peppers
2   tablespoons unsalted butter
1   large yellow onion, cut into ½-inch dice
2   teaspoons minced garlic
1   package (8 ounces) Neufchatel cream cheese,
     cut into 8 pieces
2   cups finely chopped ripe tomatoes
¼   cup finely chopped fresh cilantro
1¾ cups grated Monterey Jack cheese
8   flour tortillas (8 to 10 inches)
1   can (15 ounces) black beans, drained
2   cups good-quality tomato salsa

**1.** Prepare a two-zone fire for medium heat (see pages 14-15).

**2.** Lightly coat the chicken on both sides with oil. Season evenly with the cumin, salt, and pepper. Brush the cooking grate clean. Grill the chicken over *direct medium heat*, with the lid closed as much as possible, until the meat is firm to the touch and no longer pink in the center, 8 to 12 minutes, turning once or twice. Swap their positions as needed for even cooking. At the same time, grill the chile peppers until evenly charred on all sides, 7 to 9 minutes, turning as needed.

**3.** Place the chile peppers in a bowl and cover with plastic wrap to trap the steam. Set aside for about 10 minutes, then peel away and discard the charred skin, stems, and seeds. Cut the peppers into ¼-inch dice. Cut the chicken into ¼-inch strips.

**4.** In a medium saucepan over medium heat, melt the butter. Cook the onion until soft, about 5 minutes, stirring occasionally. Add the garlic and cook for another 2 to 3 minutes. Add the cream cheese. Stir constantly until the cheese has a smooth consistency. Add the diced peppers, tomatoes, and chicken. Mix well and continue to cook for 5 minutes. Add the cilantro and remove from the heat.

**5.** Spread a layer of grated cheese over each tortilla, keeping a 1-inch border around the edges. Then add some of the chicken mixture and black beans. Fold the sides over the filling, then roll up the tortilla to enclose the filling. Grill the burritos, seam sides down first, over *direct medium heat*, with the lid open, until the cheese is melted and the tortillas are well marked, about 2 minutes, turning carefully as needed. Serve warm with salsa.

**Makes 8 burritos**

# Grilled Chicken, Smoked Gouda, and Arugula Panini

**Prep time: 15 minutes**
**Grilling time: 6 to 10 minutes**

    4  boneless, skinless chicken breast halves
       (without tenders), 4 to 5 ounces each
       Extra virgin olive oil
    1  teaspoon prepared chili powder
    1  teaspoon kosher salt
    ½  teaspoon freshly ground black pepper
    3  tablespoons mayonnaise
    2  tablespoons Dijon mustard
    8  slices country-style white bread, about ½ inch thick
    2  cups lightly packed baby arugula leaves
    4  thin slices smoked Gouda cheese

**1.** Prepare a two-zone fire for high heat (see pages 14-15).

**2.** Between 2 sheets of plastic wrap, pound the chicken breasts to an even ½-inch thickness. Lightly coat them on both sides with oil. Season evenly with the chili powder, salt, and pepper. Brush the cooking grate clean. Grill the chicken over ***direct high heat***, with the lid closed as much as possible, until the meat is slightly firm and no longer pink in the center, 3 to 5 minutes, turning once and swapping their positions as needed for even cooking.

**3.** In a small bowl mix the mayonnaise and mustard.

**4.** On a large baking sheet arrange the bread slices in a single layer. Brush one side with olive oil and turn them over. Lightly coat the sides facing up with the mayonnaise mixture. Build the sandwiches with the grilled chicken, arugula, and cheese, and top with the remaining bread slices. Press down to make compact sandwiches. *Note: The sandwiches may be made up to this point a couple hours before you plan to serve. Keep them covered with plastic wrap in the refrigerator.*

Pound chicken breasts to an even thickness between two pieces of plastic wrap.

**5.** Place the sandwiches over ***direct low heat***. Place a baking sheet on top and weigh it down with something heavy, such as a cast-iron pan or bricks. Leave the grill's lid open. Cook until both sides of the sandwiches are golden brown and the cheese is melted, 3 to 5 minutes, turning once by carefully removing the weight and the baking sheet before turning with a spatula and swapping their positions as needed for even cooking. Then return the baking sheet and weight in place. Remove the sandwiches from the grill and cut in halves or quarters. Serve warm.

**Makes 4 servings**

# Chinese Chicken Salad

**Prep time: 30 minutes**
**Grilling time: 8 to 12 minutes**

**Salad**

  2  boneless, skinless chicken breast halves,
      6 to 8 ounces each
  1  tablespoon peanut oil
  ½  teaspoon pure chile powder
  ½  teaspoon kosher salt
  ¼  teaspoon freshly ground black pepper
  1  cup coarsely shredded carrots
      (about 2 medium carrots)
  1  cup roughly chopped cashews
  1  cup bean sprouts
  ⅓  cup thinly sliced scallions, white and light green parts
  ¼  cup finely chopped fresh chives

**Dressing**

  2  tablespoons peanut oil
  1  tablespoon rice vinegar
  2  teaspoons honey
  1  teaspoon soy sauce
  1  teaspoon black bean sauce with garlic
  1  teaspoon minced garlic
  1  teaspoon finely grated fresh ginger
  ½  teaspoon dark sesame oil
  ⅛  teaspoon dry mustard powder
  ⅛  teaspoon freshly ground black pepper

**1.** Prepare a two-zone fire for medium heat (see pages 14-15).

**2.** Lightly coat the chicken with oil. Season evenly with the chile powder, salt, and pepper. Brush the cooking grate clean. Grill the chicken over ***direct medium heat***, with the lid closed as much as possible, until the meat is firm to the touch and no longer pink in the center, 8 to 12 minutes, turning once or twice. Swap their positions as needed for even cooking. Remove from the grill and let cool until you can handle the meat with your fingers.

**3.** Using your fingers, pull the meat apart into shreds roughly ¼ inch thick and 1 to 2 inches long. Place in a large bowl. Add the remaining salad ingredients. Mix well.

**4.** In a small bowl whisk the dressing ingredients until emulsified. Add enough dressing to the salad to lightly coat the ingredients. Mix well. Serve immediately or cover with plastic wrap and refrigerate for as long as 8 hours. Serve at room temperature.

**Makes 4 servings**

# Rosemary Chicken Breasts with Black Olive Aioli

**Prep time: 15 minutes**
**Marinating time: 1 to 2 hours**
**Grilling time: 8 to 12 minutes**

### Paste
¼ cup extra virgin olive oil
1 tablespoon minced fresh rosemary
1 tablespoon Dijon mustard
1 tablespoon fresh lemon juice
2 teaspoons minced garlic
1 teaspoon kosher salt
½ teaspoon ground fennel seed
¼ teaspoon freshly ground black pepper

4 boneless, skinless chicken breast halves, about 6 ounces each

### Sauce
½ cup mayonnaise
2 tablespoons black olive tapenade
1 tablespoon fresh lemon juice
1 teaspoon finely chopped fresh rosemary
¼ teaspoon freshly ground black pepper

**1.** In a small bowl mix the paste ingredients. Reserve the woody stems of the rosemary branches to add to the charcoal. Put the chicken breasts on a plate. Coat them on both sides with the paste. Cover and refrigerate for 1 to 2 hours.

**2.** In a small bowl whisk the sauce ingredients until smooth. Cover and refrigerate until 30 minutes before serving.

**3.** Prepare a two-zone fire for medium heat (see pages 14-15).

**4.** Brush the cooking grate clean. Toss the rosemary branches onto the lit charcoal. Grill the chicken over ***direct medium heat***, with the lid closed as much as possible, until the meat is firm to the touch and no longer pink in the center, 8 to 12 minutes, turning once or twice and swapping their positions as needed for even cooking. Remove from the grill and serve warm or at room temperature with the sauce.

**Makes 4 servings**

# Chicken, Sausage, and Shrimp Paella

**Prep time: 25 minutes**
**Grilling time: about 1 hour**

**Broth**

- 1 cup ½-inch-diced yellow onion
- 1½ tablespoons thinly sliced garlic
- 2 tablespoons extra virgin olive oil
- 1 tablespoon tomato paste
- 1 bay leaf
- ¼ teaspoon paprika
- ¼ teaspoon dried oregano
- 6 cups low-sodium chicken broth
- ¼ teaspoon kosher salt
- ¼ teaspoon crumbled saffron threads

- 4 boneless, skinless chicken thighs, 3 to 4 ounces each
- 4 tablespoons extra virgin olive oil, divided
- ½ teaspoon kosher salt
- ¼ teaspoon freshly ground black pepper
- 2 large hot Italian sausages, about 6 ounces each
- 1 large red bell pepper, cut into ½-inch pieces
- 1 large green bell pepper, cut into ½-inch pieces
- 1½ cups Arborio rice
- ½ pound medium shrimp (about 15), shell on and deveined
- 1 tablespoon roughly chopped Italian parsley

**1.** Prepare a two-zone fire for high heat (see pages 14-15).

**2.** In a medium ovenproof saucepan over *direct high heat*, cook the onion and garlic with the oil until the onion is translucent but not browned, 3 to 5 minutes, stirring often. Add the tomato paste, bay leaf, paprika, and oregano. Stir with the onion for about 1 minute. Add the chicken broth, salt, and saffron. Cover the saucepan. When the liquid comes to a boil, remove the lid and slide the saucepan toward the middle of the cooking grate. Cook at a simmer for about 5 minutes. Remove the bay leaf. Cover the saucepan and carefully set aside, off the grill, while you grill the chicken and sausages.

**3.** Lightly coat the chicken on both sides with 2 tablespoons of the olive oil. Season evenly with the salt and pepper. Brush the cooking grate clean. Grill the chicken over *direct high heat*, with the lid closed as much as possible, until lightly charred on both sides but still a little undercooked, 4 to 6 minutes, turning once and swapping their positions as needed for even cooking. At the same time, grill the sausages over *indirect high heat* until firm, 8 to 12 minutes, turning occasionally and swapping their positions as needed for even cooking. Move the chicken and sausages to a cutting board and chop into ¾-inch pieces.

**4.** At this point, to cook the paella, you may need to add more charcoal to the fire for high heat.

**5.** When the fire is ready, place a 12-inch, cast-iron pan over *direct high heat*. Add the remaining 2 tablespoons of olive oil to the pan and, when it is warmed but not at smoking point, add the bell peppers. Cook in the hot oil, stirring from time to time, until they begin to soften, 3 to 4 minutes. Add about 5 cups of broth to the pan. Scatter the rice around the entire area of the pan, making sure that all of it is immersed in the broth. Slide the pan to the part of the cooking grate where the liquid will simmer slowly. Cover the grill and let the rice cook for 15 minutes, rotating the pan once or twice for even cooking.

**6.** Bury the chicken and sausages in the rice and broth. If the rice looks dry, add the remaining broth. Stir once to make sure the rice is not sticking to the pan. Cover the grill again and let the paella cook until the rice is al dente, about 10 minutes, rotating the pan once.

**7.** Then bury the shrimp in the rice, stir briefly, close the grill's lid again, and cook until the shrimp are barely done and the rice at the bottom turns a little crispy, 5 to 7 minutes. Carefully remove the pan from the grill. Garnish with chopped parsley. Taste the rice and, if necessary, add salt and pepper. Let cool for 5 minutes before serving.

**Makes 4 to 6 servings**

# Slow-Grilled Tequila-Citrus Chicken Thighs

**Prep time: 10 minutes**
**Marinating time: 6 to 8 hours**
**Grilling time: 30 to 40 minutes**

**Marinade**
- ½ cup fresh orange juice
- ¼ cup tequila
- 2 tablespoons fresh lime juice
- 2 tablespoons extra virgin olive oil
- 1 tablespoon Tabasco® chipotle pepper sauce
- 1 tablespoon roughly chopped garlic
- 1½ teaspoons kosher salt
- 1 teaspoon dried oregano
- ¼ teaspoon freshly ground black pepper

- 8 chicken thighs (with bone and skin),
  5 to 6 ounces each, trimmed of excess fat and skin

**1.** In a medium bowl mix the marinade ingredients. Put the chicken thighs in a large, resealable plastic bag and pour in the marinade. Press the air out of the bag and seal tightly. Turn the bag to distribute the marinade, lay flat in a rimmed dish, and refrigerate for 6 to 8 hours, turning once.

**2.** Prepare a two-zone fire for low heat (see pages 14-15).

**3.** Remove the chicken thighs from the bag and pour the marinade into a small saucepan. Bring the marinade to a boil and let it boil for at least 30 seconds to kill any raw chicken bacteria. Let the chicken sit at room temperature for 20 to 30 minutes before grilling.

**4.** Brush the cooking grate clean. Grill the chicken, skin side down first, over *direct low heat*, with the lid closed as much as possible, until the meat is firm and no longer pink near the bone, 30 to 40 minutes, turning every 5 minutes and swapping their positions as needed for even cooking. During the last 20 minutes of grilling, brush the chicken on both sides with the boiled marinade. Serve warm or at room temperature.

**Makes 4 servings**

---

# Hong Kong Barbecued Chicken

**Prep time: 10 minutes**
**Marinating time: 2 hours**
**Grilling time: 30 to 40 minutes**

- 4 chicken thighs (with bone and skin),
  5 to 6 ounces each, trimmed of excess fat and skin
- 4 chicken drumsticks, 3 to 4 ounces each
- 1 teaspoon kosher salt
- ½ teaspoon freshly ground black pepper

**Sauce**
- 2 tablespoons hoisin sauce
- 2 tablespoons cider vinegar
- 1 tablespoon plus 1 teaspoon Dijon mustard
- 2 teaspoons soy sauce
- 2 teaspoons peanut oil
- ¼ teaspoon freshly ground black pepper

**1.** Season the chicken evenly on both sides with the salt and pepper. Cover and refrigerate for up to 2 hours. Let the chicken sit at room temperature for 20 to 30 minutes before grilling.

**2.** In a small bowl whisk the sauce ingredients until smooth.

**3.** Prepare a two-zone fire for medium heat (see pages 14-15).

**4.** Brush the cooking grate clean. Grill the chicken, skin side down first, over *direct medium heat*, with the lid closed as much as possible, until golden brown, about 10 minutes, turning occasionally and swapping their positions as needed for even cooking.

**5.** Move the chicken pieces over *indirect medium heat* and cook for about 10 minutes, with the lid closed. Then brush both sides with a thin layer of the sauce. Continue cooking over *indirect medium heat*, with the lid closed as much as possible, until the juices run clear and the meat is no longer pink at the bone, 10 to 20 minutes more, turning and brushing with the sauce occasionally, and swapping their positions as needed for even cooking. Serve warm or at room temperature.

**Makes 4 servings**

Slow-grilled Tequila-Citrus Chicken Thighs

Hong Kong Barbecued Chicken

## ANDY GRIFFITH

Obviously this Andy Griffith is not the actor who played Matlock or Mayberry's laid-back sheriff on television. Instead, he is a charcoal grilling zealot with little patience for pale imitations of jerk chicken. "I'm sorry," he says, "but slightly spicy chicken breasts grilled over gas don't even come close to the mind-blowing chicken I've had at some jerk huts in Jamaica." As a young man growing up in South Wales, Andy vacationed from time to time in the Caribbean. "There," he says, "the crazy, smoky flavor goes right to the bone, and the taste of all the ingredients is electric."

If you cut a few slashes in each piece of chicken, the marinade flavors and smoke will get all the way to the bone.

Andy begins his rendition of jerk chicken with a wet marinade over drumsticks and thighs (no breasts, please). The really important flavors here are allspice, thyme, and, of course, the chiles! Don't skimp on the chiles. Yes, this chicken is spicy. "No worries," Andy says. "With some cold beer and a hanky, you will be fine."

In Jamaica, jerk is traditionally cooked over branches of pimento (allspice). Andy recommends apple wood as a suitable substitute, provided you have sufficient allspice flavor in the marinade. He smokes his chicken at low temperatures for a couple hours, after which time you can slurp the meat right off the bone, though the skin gets a little rubbery. To give the skin a crackling crisp texture, he finishes the chicken over a hot fire, reheating it at the same time if it has been held in the refrigerator for several hours.

# Andy's Jerk Chicken

**Prep time: 25 minutes**
**Marinating time: 12 to 16 hours**
**Grilling time: 1¾ to 2 hours**

## Marinade
- ½ cup fresh orange juice
- ½ cup fresh lime juice
- 1 bunch (8 to 10) scallions, white and light green parts, roughly chopped
- 2-3 habanero or Scotch bonnet chiles, stemmed and seeded
- 3 large garlic cloves, roughly chopped
- 1 tablespoon fresh thyme leaves (or 2 teaspoons dried thyme)
- 1 tablespoon ground allspice
- 1 tablespoon kosher salt
- 2 teaspoons freshly ground black pepper
- 1 teaspoon ground cinnamon
- 1 teaspoon dry mustard
- ¼ teaspoon freshly grated nutmeg

<br>

- 3 pounds bone-in chicken pieces (drumsticks and thighs)
- 2 large handfuls apple wood chips (or 2 large chunks), soaked in water for at least 30 minutes

**1.** In a blender or food processor, combine the marinade ingredients and process for about 1 minute (use rubber gloves when handling the chiles). The solids should be pulverized.

**2.** Trim and discard any excess fat hanging from the edges of the chicken. Using a sharp knife, cut a few shallow slashes in each piece of chicken to let the flavors of the marinade and the smoke seep inside. Place the chicken on a large, rimmed baking sheet. Use a spoon to smear the marinade all over the chicken. Cover with plastic wrap and refrigerate for 12 to 16 hours.

**3.** Prepare a two-zone fire for low heat (see pages 14-15). Push the charcoal all the way to one side so it doesn't cover more than one-third of the charcoal grate. If you have a smoker, set it up for a heat range of 225˚F to 250˚F, according to the manufacturer's directions. Drain and add about half of the wood chips (or 1 chunk) to the charcoal.

**4.** Remove the chicken from the baking sheet and let sit at room temperature for 20 to 30 minutes before grilling. Pour the marinade into a small saucepan. Keep it refrigerated while the chicken cooks for the first hour.

**5.** Brush the cooking grate clean. When the wood begins to smoke, grill the chicken, skin side down, over ***indirect low heat***, with the lid closed as much as possible, for 1 hour. At this point, if you are using a charcoal grill (not a smoker), you may need to add 8 to 10 unlit charcoal briquettes (or an equivalent amount of lump charcoal) to the fire to maintain the heat.

**6.** Bring the marinade to a boil and let it boil for at least 30 seconds to kill any raw chicken bacteria. Brush the marinade all over the chicken. Turn the chicken skin side up. Drain and add the remaining wood chips (or chunk) and continue to grill, with the lid closed as much as possible, until the chicken is fully cooked, 45 minutes to 1 hour. At this point the meat will be tender but the skin will be rubbery. Remove from the grill. Cover and refrigerate until 30 to 60 minutes before serving.

**7.** Prepare a two-zone fire for medium heat (see pages 14-15).

**8.** To crisp the skin, grill the chicken, skin side down first, over ***direct medium heat***, with the lid closed as much as possible, until warm and well browned on all sides, 5 to 10 minutes, turning once or twice and swapping their positions as needed for even cooking. Serve warm.

**Makes 4 to 6 servings**

# Tripp's Chicken with White Barbecue Sauce

**Prep time: 15 minutes**
**Grilling time: 30 to 40 minutes**

**Sauce**

- 1 large yellow onion
- 2 medium garlic cloves
- 4 tablespoons unsalted butter, cut into 4 pieces
- ½ cup dry white wine
- 1 cup Miracle Whip® dressing
- ⅓ cup loosely packed, roughly chopped fresh tarragon
- ¼ cup apple cider vinegar (5% acidity)
- 2 tablespoons fresh lemon juice
- 1 tablespoon Dijon mustard
- 1 tablespoon granulated sugar
- ½ teaspoon Texas Pete® hot sauce
- 1 teaspoon sea salt
- 1 teaspoon coarsely ground black pepper

- 16 chicken drumsticks, 3 to 4 ounces each
  Vegetable oil
- 2 teaspoons kosher salt
- ½ teaspoon freshly ground black pepper

**1.** Mince the onion and garlic until they are almost a paste. In a medium saucepan over medium heat, melt the butter. Add the onion and garlic and cook until the mixture is opaque, 2 to 3 minutes, stirring occasionally. Add the white wine. Mix well and cook until half of the liquid has evaporated, 2 to 3 minutes, stirring occasionally. Remove the pan from the heat and let cool for about 5 minutes. Whisk in the remaining sauce ingredients. The sauce should have the consistency of ranch dressing. Cover and refrigerate until about 1 hour before serving.

**2.** Prepare a two-zone fire for medium heat (see pages 14-15). Let the chicken sit at room temperature for 20 to 30 minutes before grilling. Lightly coat the chicken on all sides with oil. Season evenly with the salt and pepper.

**3.** Brush the cooking grate clean. Grill the chicken over ***indirect medium heat***, with the lid closed as much as possible, until the juices run clear and the meat is opaque all the way to the bone, 30 to 40 minutes, turning occasionally and swapping positions for even cooking.

**4.** During the last 5 to 10 minutes of cooking, lightly brush the chicken with the sauce. Serve warm with more sauce on the side. Refrigerate remaining sauce for up to 2 weeks.

**Makes 4 to 6 servings**

My friend Tripp is a Southerner who grew up eating barbecue with white sauce. That's right, white sauce, because it is based on mayonnaise or Miracle Whip® dressing. He has taken the basic recipe, which is famous all over Alabama, to new heights with the addition of white wine and tarragon.

# Bourbon-Barbecued Duck Legs

**Prep time: 10 minutes**
**Grilling time: 45 to 60 minutes**

**Sauce**
½ cup ketchup
¼ cup aged bourbon
2 tablespoons light brown sugar
1 tablespoon molasses
1 tablespoon Worcestershire sauce
1 tablespoon Dijon mustard
1 tablespoon cider vinegar
½ teaspoon granulated onion
½ teaspoon kosher salt
¼ teaspoon Chinese five-spice powder, optional

6 whole duck legs (with thighs attached),
  8 to 10 ounces each
2 teaspoons kosher salt
1 teaspoon prepared chili powder
1 teaspoon freshly ground black pepper

**1.** In a small saucepan whisk the sauce ingredients with ¼ cup of water. Bring the sauce to a boil briefly over high heat, then reduce the heat and simmer the sauce for a minute or so.

**2.** Season the duck legs evenly with the salt, chili powder, and pepper. Let the duck sit at room temperature for 20 to 30 minutes before grilling.

**3.** Prepare a two-zone fire for high heat (see pages 14-15). Lay a large, disposable drip pan on the empty side of the charcoal grate.

**4.** Brush the cooking grate clean. Grill the duck legs, skin side down, over *indirect high heat*, with the lid closed as much as possible, for 30 minutes. Then spread 8 to 10 charcoal briquettes (or an equivalent amount of lump charcoal) over the lit charcoal. Turn the duck legs over and swap their positions as needed for even cooking. Continue to grill, with the lid closed as much as possible, until the meat is no longer red at the bone and the internal temperature reaches 175°F. The total grilling time will be 45 to 60 minutes. During the final 10 minutes, lightly brush the duck on all sides with the sauce. Serve warm.

**Makes 6 servings**

# Grilled Duck Breasts with Asian Rub and Mustard Dipping Sauce

**Prep time: 25 minutes**
**Grilling time: 9 to 12 minutes**

**Rub**

|  |  |
|---|---|
| 1 | tablespoon paprika |
| 1 | teaspoon kosher salt |
| 1 | teaspoon ground coriander |
| 1 | teaspoon Chinese five-spice powder |
| ½ | teaspoon ground ginger |
| ¼ | teaspoon ground allspice |
| ¼ | teaspoon ground cayenne pepper |

4  boneless Muscovy duck breast halves (with skin), 10 to 12 ounces each and about 1 inch thick

**Sauce**

|  |  |
|---|---|
| ¼ | cup Dijon mustard |
| 2 | tablespoons soy sauce |
| 1 | teaspoon honey |
| ¼ | teaspoon hot chili oil |

1  handful apple wood chips, soaked in water for at least 30 minutes

**1.** In a small bowl mix the rub ingredients. With a sharp knife, score the skin of the duck breasts in a diamond pattern. Cut through the fat but not into the meat. Trim any excess skin that hangs over the edges. Season the breasts evenly with the rub and let sit at room temperature for 20 to 30 minutes before grilling.

Scoring the skin in a diamond pattern helps the fat to render. Trim any excess skin that hangs over the edges.

**2.** Prepare a three-zone sloped fire for high heat (see page 16).

**3.** In a small bowl whisk the sauce ingredients.

**4.** Drain the wood chips and scatter them over the charcoal. Brush

Grilling the skin side first over the outer edges of the charcoal, where flare-ups are less likely, renders out some fat and crisps the skin.

the cooking grate clean. When the chips begin to smoke, place the duck breasts, skin side down, over the area with just a single layer of charcoal. This placement will begin to melt the fat and crisp the skin with a low risk of flare-ups. Grill the breasts, with the lid closed as much as possible, until dark brown on the skin side, 3 to 4 minutes, swapping and rotating their positions as needed for even cooking. Then turn the breasts over so they are skin side up, and grill them over ***direct high heat***, with the lid closed as much as possible, until well marked on the second side, 3 to 4 minutes. If flare-ups occur, move the breasts temporarily over indirect heat. To finish, move the breasts to the other side of the grill, as close as possible to the charcoal but not directly over it. Cook over ***indirect high heat***, with the lid closed as much as possible, until the duck is medium rare, 3 to 4 minutes, turning once. Remove the breasts from the grill, loosely cover with foil, and let rest for 3 to 4 minutes. Cut the duck breasts crosswise on the bias. Serve warm with the dipping sauce.

**Makes 4 to 6 servings**

# JOHN GERALD GLEESON

About 220 miles north of Detroit's hustle and bustle, on the edge of a pristine little lake, John Gleeson is happily retired from a successful career as an attorney. In his spare time, he has developed a knack for choosing the right kind of charcoal to burn for various types of food. For example, in this recipe he prefers briquettes because of the way they burn quite hot at the start and slowly lose heat over time (100 degrees or more over the course of an hour). Lump charcoal loses heat much more quickly, meaning you need to add charcoal more often if you want to sustain the fire for a long period. John chooses lump charcoal (it has more flavor) for quick-grilling foods like steaks and chops, but for anything that requires more than 30 minutes he uses briquettes, often in combination with wood chips.

John's secret ingredient: dried granulated orange peel.

With poultry, John especially likes the flavor of apple wood chips. Then again, he might use the stripped branches of woody herbs like rosemary and thyme. Either way, the light smoke provides an additional layer of flavor, never so heavy that it would smother the delicate meat of game hens but just enough that you know it's there.

LIVE FIRE WISDOM
WEBER'S CHARCOAL

# John's Game Hens

**Prep time: 15 minutes**
**Grilling time: 50 to 60 minutes**

**Paste**
  5  tablespoons extra virgin olive oil
  2  tablespoons Dijon mustard
  1  tablespoon dried granulated orange peel
  2  teaspoons kosher salt
1½  teaspoons dried thyme
  1  teaspoon dried sage
  1  teaspoon marjoram
½  teaspoon freshly ground black pepper

  4  Cornish game hens, 1½ to 2 pounds each
  1  large orange, cut into 4 wedges
  1  small handful apple wood chips,
     soaked in water for at least 30 minutes

**1.** In a small bowl thoroughly mix the paste ingredients.

**2.** Remove and discard the giblets from the hens and rinse them, inside and out, under cold water. Pat dry with paper towels. Fold the wings behind the back of each hen. Spread the paste over the entire surface of the hens. Squeeze the juice of 1 orange wedge into the cavity of each hen. Stuff each orange wedge inside the cavity. Truss each hen with kitchen twine (see page 244).

**3.** Prepare a three-zone split fire for high heat (see page 17). Place a large, disposable drip pan between the two piles of charcoal.

**4.** Brush the cooking grate clean. Drain the wood chips and scatter them over one pile of charcoal. Place the hens in a line over *indirect high heat*. Cook the hens, with the lid closed as much possible, until the juices run clear and the meat is no longer pink at the bone, 50 to 60 minutes. For even browning and cooking, rotate the hens and swap their positions 2 or 3 times during cooking. When fully cooked, remove the hens from the grill and let rest for 5 to 10 minutes. Remove the strings and cut into serving pieces. Serve warm.

**Makes 4 to 6 servings**

# Southern BBQ Chicken
# with Pecan Smoke and Peach Chutney

**Prep time: 25 minutes**
**Grilling time: 1¼ to 1½ hours**

**Chutney**
- 8 ounces frozen sliced peaches
- ⅓ cup peach nectar
- ⅓ cup ketchup
- 2 tablespoons peach preserves
- 2 teaspoons cider vinegar
- 2 teaspoons prepared yellow mustard
- ½ teaspoon Worcestershire sauce
- ¼ teaspoon kosher salt
- ⅛ teaspoon ground allspice

**Rub**
- 1 teaspoon paprika
- 1 teaspoon pure chile powder
- 1 teaspoon kosher salt
- 1 teaspoon dried sage
- ½ teaspoon granulated onion
- ¼ teaspoon ground cumin
- ¼ teaspoon freshly ground black pepper

- 1 whole chicken, 4½ to 5 pounds, split in half, backbone and wing tips removed
  Extra virgin olive oil
- 1 small handful pecan wood chips (or 1 small chunk), soaked in water for at least 30 minutes

1. In a medium saucepan mix the chutney ingredients. Bring to a boil, reduce the heat to a simmer, and cook for about 10 minutes. The peaches should be very soft. Let the mixture cool. If the chutney is too thick, add another tablespoon or so of peach nectar.

2. In a small bowl mix the rub ingredients.

3. Lightly coat each half of the chicken on both sides with oil and season evenly with the rub. Let the chicken sit at room temperature for 20 to 30 minutes before grilling.

4. Prepare a two-zone fire for medium heat (see pages 14-15).

5. Drain the wood chips (or chunk) and scatter them over the charcoal. Brush the cooking grate clean. When the chips begin to smoke, place the chicken halves over *indirect medium heat*, with the breast sides facing up and the legs facing toward the charcoal. Keep the lid closed as much as possible and cook until the internal temperature registers 180˚F in the thickest part of the thigh (not touching the bone), 1¼ to 1½ hours. Rotate the chicken as needed for even cooking and browning.

6. To maintain the heat, add 10 to 12 unlit charcoal briquettes (or an equivalent amount of lump charcoal) to the fire every 30 to 45 minutes. During the last 5 to 10 minutes of cooking, lightly brush the skin side of the chicken halves with some chutney. When fully cooked, remove the chicken from the grill and let rest for 5 to 10 minutes. Cut into serving pieces. Serve warm with the chutney on the side.

**Makes 4 servings**

# Smoked Chicken

**Prep time: 10 minutes**
**Salt-curing time: 1½ to 2 hours**
**Grilling time: 1¼ to 1½ hours**

  1  whole chicken, 4 to 4½ pounds
  ¼  cup plus ½ teaspoon kosher salt, divided
1½  tablespoons unsalted butter, melted
  ½  teaspoon freshly ground black pepper
  1  large handful oak wood chips, soaked in water
     for at least 30 minutes

**1.** Remove and discard the neck, giblets, and any excess fat from the chicken. Fold the wing tips behind the chicken's back. Use ¼ cup of the salt to sprinkle over the entire surface and inside the cavity of the chicken, covering it all like a light blanket of snow. Cover the chicken with plastic wrap and refrigerate for 1½ to 2 hours.

**2.** Rinse the chicken inside and out with cold water. Gently pat the chicken dry with paper towels. Brush the surface with the butter. Season with the remaining ½ teaspoon salt and the pepper. Do not truss the chicken. Let the chicken sit at room temperature for 20 to 30 minutes before grilling.

**3.** Prepare a two-zone fire for medium heat (see pages 14-15).

**4.** Drain the wood chips and scatter them over the charcoal. Brush the cooking grate clean. When the chips begin to smoke, place the chicken, breast side up, over *indirect medium heat*, with the legs facing the side of the grill with charcoal. Keep the lid closed as much as possible and cook until the internal temperature registers 180°F in the thickest part of the thigh (not touching the bone),

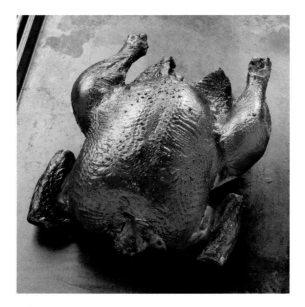

Salt-curing and then smoking the chicken gives the skin a rich mahogany color.

1¼ to 1½ hours. Rotate the chicken as needed for even cooking and browning. To maintain the heat, add 10 to 12 unlit charcoal briquettes (or an equivalent amount of lump charcoal) to the fire every 30 to 45 minutes.

**5.** When fully cooked, remove the chicken from the grill and let rest for about 10 minutes. Cut into serving pieces, or slice the meat and prepare a sandwich, as in the photo to the right. Serve warm or at room temperature.

**Makes 2 to 4 servings**

# Garlic and Oregano Beer Can Chicken

**Prep time: 15 minutes**
**Marinating time: 2 to 4 hours**
**Grilling time: 1 to 1½ hours**

  4  small garlic cloves
  2  teaspoons dried oregano
  1  teaspoon kosher salt
  ½  teaspoon crushed red pepper flakes
  1  tablespoon vegetable oil
  2  teaspoons fresh lime juice
  1  whole chicken, 3½ to 4 pounds
  1  can (12 ounces) beer, at room temperature

**1.** Using a mortar and pestle, pound the garlic, oregano, salt, and red pepper flakes into a paste as smooth as possible. Add the oil and lime juice. Mix until all the ingredients are evenly distributed.

**2.** Remove and discard the neck, giblets, and any excess fat from the chicken. Rinse the chicken, inside and out, under cold water. Pat dry with paper towels. Coat the chicken all over with the paste. Cover and refrigerate for 2 to 4 hours.

**3.** Prepare a three-zone split fire for medium heat (see page 17). Place a large, disposable drip pan between the piles of charcoal and fill it about halfway with warm water.

**4.** Let the chicken sit at room temperature for 20 to 30 minutes before grilling. Open the beer can and pour out (or drink) about half the beer. Using a can opener, make 2 more holes in the top of the can. Place the can on a solid surface. Plunk the chicken cavity over the can.

**5.** Transfer the chicken-on-a-can to the grill, balancing the two legs and the can like a tripod. Fold the wing tips behind the chicken's back. Grill over ***indirect medium heat***, with the lid closed as much as possible, until the juices run clear and the internal temperature registers 180°F in the thickest part of the thigh (not touching the bone), 1 to 1½ hours, carefully rotating as needed for even cooking. To maintain the heat, you may need to add 5 to 6 unlit charcoal briquettes (or an equivalent amount of lump charcoal) to each pile of charcoal every 30 to 45 minutes. Carefully remove the chicken-on-a-can from the grill. Do not spill contents of the very hot beer can! Let the chicken rest for about 10 minutes before lifting it from the can and cutting it into serving pieces. Serve warm.

**Makes 2 to 4 servings**

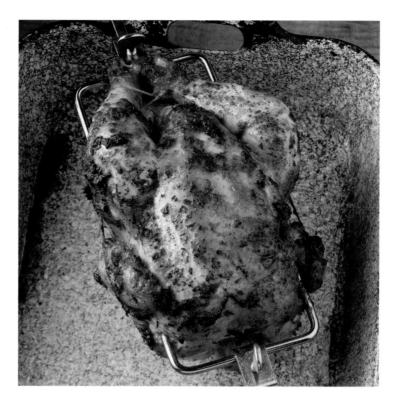

# Lemon-Curry Rotisserie Chicken

**Prep time: 10 minutes**
**Marinating time: 8 to 12 hours**
**Grilling time: 1 to 1½ hours**

**Marinade**
  Grated zest and juice of 1 lemon
2  teaspoons extra virgin olive oil
1  teaspoon curry powder
1  teaspoon Dijon mustard
1  teaspoon dried thyme
1  teaspoon granulated garlic
¾  teaspoon kosher salt
½  teaspoon ground cayenne pepper

1  whole chicken, 3½ to 4 pounds

**1.** In a medium bowl mix the marinade ingredients until you create a paste. Remove the wing tips, giblets, and any excess fat from the chicken. Rinse the chicken, inside and out, under cold water, pat dry with paper towels, and place in a large bowl. Spread the paste all over the outside of the chicken. Cover the bowl and refrigerate for 8 to 12 hours.

**2.** Prepare a three-zone split fire for medium heat (see page 17), using mesquite lump charcoal. Place a large, disposable drip pan between the piles of charcoal and fill it about halfway with warm water.

**3.** Truss the chicken with kitchen twine (see page 244). Following the grill's instructions, secure the chicken in the middle of a rotisserie, put the rotisserie in place, and turn it on. Cook the chicken over *indirect medium heat*, with the lid closed as much as possible, until the internal temperature reaches 180°F in the thickest part of the thigh (not touching the bone), 1 to 1½ hours. To maintain the heat, you may need to add 5 to 6 unlit charcoal briquettes (or an equivalent amount of lump charcoal) to each pile of charcoal every 30 to 45 minutes.

**4.** When the chicken is fully cooked, turn off the rotisserie and, using insulated mitts, remove the rotisserie from the grill. Tilt the chicken upright over the disposable drip pan so that the liquid that has accumulated in the chicken's cavity pours into the pan. Slide the chicken from the rotisserie onto a cutting board. Let rest for about 10 minutes before carving into serving pieces. Serve warm.

**Makes 2 to 4 servings**

# Turkey Burgers with Scallions and Mushrooms

**Prep time: 25 minutes**
**Chilling time: 2 to 3 hours**
**Grilling time: 10 to 14 minutes**

  8  ounces fresh shiitake mushrooms
  2  tablespoons thinly sliced garlic
  ¼  cup olive oil, plus a little more for grilling the patties
  1  tablespoon minced fresh ginger
  1  cup thinly sliced scallions
1¼  teaspoons kosher salt, divided
  ½  teaspoon freshly ground black pepper, divided
2½  pounds ground turkey (93% lean)
  1  tablespoon minced fresh thyme
  1  tablespoon soy sauce
  2  teaspoons dark sesame oil
  2  teaspoons dry mustard powder
  8  sesame seed buns
     Dijon mustard, optional
     Tabasco® sauce, optional

**1.** Wipe the mushrooms with a damp paper towel. Twist out the stems from the caps and discard. Cut the mushrooms into ¼-inch dice.

**2.** In a skillet large enough to hold the mushrooms in a single layer, heat the garlic in the oil over medium heat. When the garlic starts to sizzle, stir it for even cooking until it starts to turn golden, about 3 minutes. Add the ginger and the scallions and continue to cook until the scallions start to wilt, about 1 minute. With a slotted spoon, move the ingredients to a baking sheet, keeping as much of the fragrant oil as possible in the pan. Add the mushrooms in an even layer to the pan and season with ½ teaspoon salt and ¼ teaspoon pepper. Increase the heat to medium and cook until caramelized, 6 to 8 minutes, stirring occasionally. Transfer the mushrooms to the baking sheet, spreading them out to cool.

**3.** In a large bowl gently mix the turkey, cooked vegetables, thyme, soy sauce, sesame oil, mustard powder, the remaining ¾ teaspoon salt, and remaining ¼ teaspoon pepper. Divide the turkey mixture into 8 portions, about 6 ounces each. Gently shape into patties about 4 inches in diameter and ¾ inch thick. Cover and refrigerate for 2 to 3 hours.

**4.** Prepare a two-zone fire for high heat (see pages 14-15).

**5.** Lightly coat the patties on both sides with olive oil. Brush the cooking grate clean. Grill the patties over ***direct high heat***, with the lid closed as much as possible, until well browned on both sides, 6 to 8 minutes, turning once when the patties release easily from the grate and swapping their positions as needed for even cooking. Move the patties over ***indirect high heat*** and cook until the internal temperature reaches 165°F, 4 to 6 minutes, swapping their positions as needed for even cooking.

**6.** Grill the buns, cut sides down, over direct heat, with the lid open, until lightly toasted, 20 to 30 seconds. Serve warm with mustard and Tabasco® sauce, if desired.

**Makes 8 servings**

# HOW TO
# BARBECUE A TURKEY

LIVE FIRE WISDOM

Several years ago, I converted from tasteless turkeys roasted in an oven to lightly smoked turkeys done on the grill. At first my method on the grill closely resembled what I had always done with the oven—325°F for about 15 minutes per pound. The results were pretty good, because of the woodsy aromas, but I still struggled with the fact that the breast meat was overcooked before the leg meat was done. Then I discovered brines, flavorful saltwater solutions that soak into the turkey and add enough moisture that you can cook the breast meat to higher temperatures than usual before it turns dry.

My next step in the right direction was to cook the breast meat more slowly than the leg meat. How? I start by cooking the turkey with the breast meat facing down in a pan of liquid. This way, the leg meat gets a head start, while the breast meat is shielded from the heat by the pan and the liquid. After an hour or so, I turn the turkey over to let the breast meat and leg meat finish together—both beautifully smoked and succulent. Oh, and by the way, the liquid that protects the breast meat makes outstanding gravy.

By arranging the charcoal in a half-circle on one side of the charcoal grate, you will create higher temperatures on that side. A drip pan filled with warm water will help you maintain the temperature of the fire, which ideally should be 300°F to 350°F.

## The Day Before

1. The wing tips have almost no meat and they tend to burn, so remove them at the joint with a sharp knife or poultry shears. Also remove the neck and giblets from both ends of the turkey. Reserve all of these turkey parts for the gravy.

2. To brine the turkey, arrange it, breast side down, in a sturdy plastic bag. Put the bag in a cooler lined with ice. Then pour the brine over the turkey.

3. Pull up the sides of the bag against the turkey so the brine almost completely covers the turkey. It is important that the breast is submerged. If part of the back is not, that's okay. No one eats the back, right?

174

# Barbecuing the Turkey

1. In a heavy-duty roasting pan, combine good-quality chicken stock with aromatic vegetables and the reserved turkey parts. Place the brined turkey, breast side down, in the liquid. Place the pan over indirect low heat and add wood chips to the lit charcoal for a lightly smoked flavor.

2. After the first hour of cooking, the turkey legs, wings, and back will be golden brown, but the breast will have barely begun to cook. Turn the turkey over and finish cooking it with the breast side facing up.

3. If any parts of the turkey turn dark, cover them with foil. Remove the turkey from the grill when the internal temperature reaches 175°F in the thickest part of a thigh (not touching the bone). Or check for doneness by cutting into the joint between the leg and body. If you see any pink meat, the turkey is not done.

# Preparing the Gravy

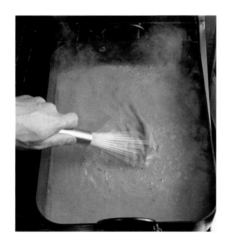

1. After removing the turkey, strain the liquid in the pan. Then cook a roux, a mixture of flour and butter, until it turns the color of peanut butter. As you pour the strained liquid over the roux, whisk vigorously to break up any lumps.

2. The gravy will not thicken fully until it comes to a boil. Continue to whisk the gravy until it boils.

3. Then lower the heat and let the gravy simmer until it reaches the consistency you like. Taste the gravy at this point and adjust the seasonings if necessary.

# Brined and Barbecued Turkey with Pan Gravy

**Prep time: 30 minutes**
**Brining time: 18 to 24 hours**
**Grilling time: 2½ to 3½ hours**

**Brine**
- 2 quarts apple juice
- 1 cup kosher salt
- 2 tablespoons dried rosemary
- 2 tablespoons dried thyme
- 1 tablespoon dried sage
- 1 teaspoon coarsely ground black pepper

- 1 turkey, 10 to 12 pounds, fresh or defrosted
- ½ cup melted unsalted butter, divided
- 1 teaspoon freshly ground black pepper
- 6 cups reduced-sodium chicken stock
- 1 large yellow onion, roughly chopped
- 2 large carrots, roughly chopped
- 2 celery stalks, roughly chopped
- 4 small chunks apple wood or 4 small handfuls apple wood chips, soaked in water for at least 30 minutes

**Gravy**
- Reserved pan liquid plus enough chicken stock to make 4 cups of liquid
- ¼ cup unsalted butter, cut into 4 equal pieces
- ¼ cup all-purpose flour
- ⅓ cup dry white wine
- 2 tablespoons finely chopped fresh Italian parsley
- Kosher salt
- Freshly ground black pepper

**1.** In a large pot combine the brine ingredients. Stir vigorously until the salt has dissolved.

**2.** Remove the neck and giblets from both ends of the turkey and reserve in the refrigerator for the gravy. Cut off and reserve the wing tips for the gravy, too. If your turkey has a trussing clamp, leave it in place. Do not truss the turkey. Rinse the turkey, inside and out, with cold water.

**3.** See the step-by-step instructions for brining the turkey on page 174. Partially fill a cooler with ice. Open a large, sturdy plastic bag in the cooler. Place the turkey, breast side down, in the bag. Carefully pour the brine over the turkey and then add 3 quarts of cold water. Press the air out of the bag, seal the bag tightly, close the lid of the cooler, and set aside for 18 to 24 hours.

**4.** Prepare a half circle or crescent-shaped fire for low heat (see page 174 for grill set up and page 15 for how to check the heat of your fire). Remove the turkey from the bag and rinse it, inside and out, with cold water. Pat dry with paper towels. Discard the brine. Lightly coat the turkey with some of the melted butter. Season with the pepper.

**5.** Pour the chicken stock into a sturdy, 9 x 13-inch roasting pan. Add the onion, carrots, and celery. Add the reserved turkey neck, giblets, and wing tips. Place the turkey, breast side down, in the roasting pan.

**6.** Place the roasting pan in the center of the cooking grate. Position the pan so the turkey legs face the charcoal. Drain, then add 2 wood chunks or 2 handfuls of wood chips to the charcoal. Cook the turkey over **_indirect low heat_** (300°F to 350°F), with the lid closed, for 1 hour.

**7.** After 1 hour, to maintain the heat, add 10 to 12 unlit charcoal briquettes to the lit charcoal, using long-handled tongs to tuck the unlit charcoal between the lit charcoal. Drain and add the remaining wood chunks or chips to the charcoal. Carefully turn the turkey over in the pan so the breast faces up. Continue to cook the turkey over _indirect low heat_, with the lid closed, for a second hour.

**8.** At the end of the second hour, baste the turkey all over with the remaining butter. If any parts are getting too dark, tightly wrap them with aluminum foil. Once again, add 10 to 12 unlit charcoal briquettes to the lit charcoal to maintain the heat. Continue to cook the turkey over _indirect low heat_. The total cooking time will be 2½ to 3½ hours. The turkey is done when the internal temperature reaches 175°F in the thickest part of the thigh (not touching the bone) and 165°F in the breast. _Note: The internal temperature will rise 5°F to 10°F during resting._

**9.** Transfer the turkey to a cutting board, loosely cover with foil, and let rest for 20 to 30 minutes before carving. Meanwhile, make the gravy.

**10.** Strain the pan liquid through a sieve into a large fat separator and discard all the solids. Add enough chicken stock to equal 4 cups of liquid. Place the roasting pan over a stovetop burner set to medium heat. Add the butter and flour. As the butter melts, stir with a wooden spoon and cook until the mixture turns the color of peanut butter, about 5 minutes, stirring frequently. Add 4 cups of the reserved pan liquid (but not the fat) plus the wine. Bring the gravy to a boil, whisking frequently to dissolve the lumps. Lower the heat and simmer the gravy for a few minutes or until it reaches the consistency you like. If the gravy gets too thick, add more chicken stock a little at a time and simmer until it reaches the right thickness. Turn off the heat. Add the parsley. Add salt and pepper to taste. Carve the turkey. Serve warm with the gravy.

**Makes 10 to 12 servings**

# F

# FISH

# Cedar-Planked Salmon with Hoisin-Mustard Glaze

**Prep time: 10 minutes**
**Grilling time: 15 to 25 minutes**

**Glaze**
- 1 tablespoon hoisin sauce
- 1 tablespoon Dijon mustard
- 1 tablespoon fresh lemon juice
- 1 tablespoon unsalted butter, melted
- ½ teaspoon dark sesame oil

- 1 large salmon fillet (with skin), 2 to 2½ pounds, about 16 inches long and ¾ inch thick
- ½ teaspoon kosher salt
- ¼ teaspoon freshly ground black pepper

- 1 untreated cedar plank, about 16 inches by 8 inches, soaked in water for at least 1 hour

Choose a pan big enough to soak the plank in water. Weigh the plank down with something heavy so it doesn't float.

**1.** Prepare a two-zone fire for medium heat (see pages 14-15).

**2.** In a small bowl mix the glaze ingredients.

**3.** Place the salmon, skin side down, on a large cutting board. Using needle-nose pliers, remove any pin bones from the salmon. Cut the salmon in half lengthwise but do not cut through the skin. Then cut the salmon crosswise to make 6 or 8 servings but, again, do not cut through the skin. Brush the glaze evenly over the salmon flesh, brushing some glaze between the individual servings. Season the top evenly with the salt and pepper.

**4.** Place the soaked plank over *direct medium heat* and close the lid. After a few minutes, when the plank crackles and smoke begins to escape from the grill, place the salmon, skin side down, in the center of the plank. Close the lid and let the salmon cook until lightly browned on the surface and opaque all the way to the center of the flesh, 15 to 25 minutes. If at any point you see a lot of smoke pouring out of the grill, use a water bottle to extinguish the flames on the wood plank. Moving the plank over indirect heat will also prevent flare-ups, but the cooking time will be longer.

**5.** Using sturdy tongs or spatulas, carefully remove the salmon and the plank from the grill together and lay it down on a heat-proof surface. Serve the salmon on the plank or pick up individual servings by sliding a spatula between the skin and flesh. Serve warm or at room temperature.

**Makes 6 to 8 servings**

# Fennel-Spiced Salmon with Gazpacho Salad

**Prep time: 25 minutes**
**Marinating time: 1 hour**
**Grilling time: 8 to 10 minutes**

### Salad
2 tablespoons extra virgin olive oil
½ cup ¼-inch-diced red onion
2 teaspoons minced garlic
2 cups ¼-inch-diced tomatoes
1 cup ¼-inch-diced zucchini squash
1 cup seeded, ¼-inch-diced cucumber
1 cup ¼-inch-diced red bell pepper
½ teaspoon kosher salt
⅛ teaspoon freshly ground black pepper
1 teaspoon balsamic vinegar
2 tablespoons finely chopped fresh dill
Tabasco® sauce

### Rub
1 teaspoon ground fennel seed
1 teaspoon kosher salt
1 teaspoon pure chile powder
½ teaspoon celery seed
½ teaspoon freshly ground black pepper

6 skinless salmon fillets, about 8 ounces each
and 1 to 1¼ inches thick
Extra virgin olive oil

**1.** In a 12-inch skillet over medium heat, warm the oil. Cook the onion until translucent but not golden, 2 to 3 minutes, stirring occasionally. Add the garlic and cook for another minute, stirring occasionally. Add the tomatoes, zucchini, cucumber, and the bell pepper. Season with the salt and pepper. Cook the mixture for about 1 minute, stirring occasionally, to draw some liquid from the tomatoes. Remove the skillet from the heat. Add the vinegar and dill. Transfer the salad mixture to a large bowl and chill in the refrigerator for about 1 hour or as long as 8 hours (more liquid will draw from the vegetables during this time). Remove the bowl from the refrigerator about 30 minutes before serving. Taste the salad and adjust the seasonings with salt, pepper, and Tabasco®.

**2.** In a small bowl mix the rub ingredients. Brush each of the salmon fillets evenly with oil. Season them on both sides with the rub. Cover and refrigerate for up to 1 hour.

**3.** Prepare a two-zone fire for high heat (see pages 14-15).

**4.** Brush the cooking grate clean. Grill the fillets over *direct high heat*, with the lid closed as much as possible, until cooked to your desired doneness, 8 to 10 minutes for medium rare, turning once after 6 to 7 minutes. Swap their positions as needed for even cooking. Serve warm with the salad, using as much or as little of the vegetable juices as you like.

**Makes 6 servings**

# Whole Brook Trout with Lemon and Rosemary

**Prep time: 20 minutes**
**Grilling time: 8 to 10 minutes**

    4  whole trout, scaled, cleaned, and boneless,
       8 to 10 ounces each
    1  teaspoon kosher salt
    ¼  teaspoon freshly ground black pepper
       Extra virgin olive oil
    2  lemons
    1  small handful rosemary branches

**1.** Prepare a two-zone fire for high heat (see pages 14-15).

**2.** Open the trout like books to expose the fillets. Season the insides with the salt and pepper. Close the trout. Lightly coat the outsides with oil.

**3.** Remove and discard the ends from the lemons. Cut the lemons crosswise into ¼-inch slices. Arrange half the slices in a single layer on one side of a grill basket (one large enough for 4 trout or two smaller baskets for

2 trout each). Place the trout on top of the lemon slices. Arrange the remaining lemon slices on top of the trout. Close and secure the basket(s), being careful not to press down too hard on the trout and tear the skin.

**4.** Remove the grill's lid and drop the rosemary branches onto the burning charcoal. Grill the trout in the basket(s) over ***direct high heat***, with the lid off, until both the lemon slices and the trout skin are lightly charred and the fillets have turned from translucent to opaque at the thickest parts, 8 to 10 minutes, turning and rotating the basket(s) as needed to cook the fish evenly.

**5.** Remove the basket(s) from the grill and open carefully. Remove and discard the lemon slices on top. Using a large spatula, carefully lift each trout from the basket(s) onto a serving plate, leaving the lemons in the basket(s). Serve warm.

**Makes 4 servings**

---

# Arctic Char with Grilled Vegetable Confetti

**Prep time: 10 minutes**
**Grilling time: 20 to 25 minutes**

**Confetti**
    2  ears corn, husked
    1  medium red onion, cut crosswise into ⅓-inch slices
       Extra virgin olive oil
    1  pint cherry tomatoes, each one quartered
    ½  cup finely chopped fresh basil leaves
    1  tablespoon champagne vinegar
    2  teaspoons minced garlic
       Kosher salt
       Freshly ground black pepper

    4  arctic char fillets (with skin), each about 8 ounces
       and 1 inch thick
    4  lemon wedges

**1.** Prepare a two-zone fire for medium heat (see pages 14-15).

**2.** Lightly coat the corn and onion slices with oil. Brush the cooking grate clean. Grill over ***direct medium heat***, with the lid closed as much as possible, until the corn is golden

brown in spots all over, 12 to 15 minutes, and the onion slices are tender, 8 to 10 minutes, turning occasionally.

**3.** To increase the fire to high heat, fill a chimney starter about ¼ full with unlit charcoal (20 to 25 briquettes or an equivalent amount of lump charcoal) and spread the unlit charcoal evenly over the lit charcoal. Leave the lid off so the new charcoal will be fully lit in 10 to 15 minutes.

**4.** When the corn is cool enough to handle, slice the kernels into a medium bowl. Roughly chop the onions and add them to the bowl. Add the remaining confetti ingredients, including salt and pepper to taste.

**5.** Thoroughly coat the fillets with oil. Season them evenly with ¾ teaspoon salt and ½ teaspoon pepper. Brush the cooking grate clean. Grill the fillets, flesh side down first, over ***direct high heat***, with the lid closed as much as possible, until barely pink in the center, 8 to 10 minutes, turning once after 5 to 6 minutes. Swap their positions as needed for even cooking. Serve warm with the vegetable confetti and lemon wedges.

**Makes 4 servings**

# Tom's Teriyaki Shark Kabobs

**Prep time: 20 minutes**
**Marinating time: 1 hour**
**Grilling time: 8 to 12 minutes**

### Marinade
- 1 cup pineapple juice
- ½ cup low-sodium soy sauce
- ½ cup finely chopped yellow onion
- 1 tablespoon dark sesame oil
- 1 tablespoon grated fresh ginger
- 1 tablespoon minced garlic
- 1 tablespoon dark brown sugar
- 1 tablespoon fresh lemon juice

- 2½ pounds thresher shark or swordfish, cut into cubes 1 to 1½ inches thick

- 3 medium bell peppers (yellow, red, and/or green)
- 2 medium yellow onions
  Vegetable oil
- 1 teaspoon Lawry's® garlic salt
- 18 wooden skewers, soaked in water for 30 minutes
- 3 tablespoons toasted sesame seeds

**1.** In a large bowl mix the marinade ingredients. Add the cubes of fish. Mix well to submerge the fish. Cover and refrigerate for about 1 hour.

**2.** Cut each of the bell peppers into 1-inch squares, discarding the stems and seeds. Quarter the onions and separate the quarters into leaves. Discard the very small leaves from the center of the onions. Combine the peppers and onions in a large mixing bowl and add just enough vegetable oil to lightly coat them. Season with the garlic salt. Mix well. Skewer the vegetables through their centers, alternating the ingredients. Do not press the vegetables together tightly, though it is okay if they are touching.

**3.** Prepare a two-zone fire for high heat (see pages 14-15).

**4.** Remove the cubes of fish from the marinade and reserve the marinade. Skewer the cubes of fish through their centers. Do not press the fish together tightly, though it is

okay if they are touching. Brush the fish generously with oil on all sides.

**5.** Pour the reserved marinade into a small saucepan. Bring to a boil over medium-high heat and let cook for 2 minutes.

**6.** Brush the cooking grate clean. Grill the vegetable skewers over *direct high heat*, with the lid closed as much as possible, until lightly charred on all sides, 4 to 6 minutes, turning occasionally and swapping their positions as needed for even cooking. Then move the vegetable skewers over indirect heat to finish cooking them and to keep them warm while you grill the fish.

**7.** Grill the fish skewers over *direct high heat*, with the lid closed as much as possible, until lightly charred on the surface but only about three-quarters done, 4 to 6 minutes, turning once and swapping their positions as needed for even cooking.

**8.** Lay the vegetable and fish skewers on a sheet pan and spoon some of the boiled marinade over them. Tightly cover with aluminum foil and keep warm for 3 to 5 minutes. Serve with a little more boiled marinade spooned over the top. Garnish with the toasted sesame seeds.

**Makes 6 servings**

# Curry-Spiced Tuna Steaks with Warm Black Bean Salad

**Prep time: 20 minutes**
**Grilling time: 8 to 10 minutes**

**Salad**
¼ cup extra virgin olive oil
½ cup finely diced yellow onion
1 teaspoon minced garlic
1 teaspoon dried oregano
4 cups roughly chopped, loosely packed fresh spinach
1 can (15 ounces) black beans, rinsed
1 tablespoon fresh lime juice
¼ teaspoon kosher salt

5 tablespoons sour cream
1 tablespoon finely chopped fresh cilantro

1¼ teaspoons kosher salt
½ teaspoon curry powder
½ teaspoon pure chile powder
¼ teaspoon freshly ground black pepper
4 albacore tuna steaks, 6 to 8 ounces each
and about 1 inch thick
Extra virgin olive oil

**1.** In a 12-inch skillet over medium heat, warm the oil. Add the onion and cook for 3 to 4 minutes, stirring occasionally. Add the garlic and oregano and cook until the garlic begins to brown, about 1 minute, stirring occasionally. Immediately add the remaining salad ingredients. Mix well, cover the skillet, and set aside.

**2.** In a small bowl mix the sour cream and cilantro.

**3.** In a small bowl mix the salt, curry powder, chile powder, and pepper. Lightly brush the tuna steaks on both sides with oil. Season them evenly with the curry powder mixture. Cover and refrigerate for up to 1 hour.

**4.** Prepare a two-zone fire for high heat (see pages 14-15).

**5.** Brush the cooking grate clean. Grill the tuna steaks over ***direct high heat***, with the lid closed as much as possible, until well marked on the surface and just turning opaque in the center, 8 to 10 minutes, turning once and swapping their positions as needed for even cooking. Meanwhile, warm the black bean salad over medium heat, stirring occasionally.

**6.** Serve warm with the black bean salad spooned over the fish and the sour cream mixture on top.

**Makes 4 servings**

# Texas Gulf Redfish with Red Chile Salsa

**Prep time: 20 minutes**
**Grilling time: 16 to 18 minutes**

### Rub

  2  teaspoons pure chile powder
  1  teaspoon kosher salt
  ½  teaspoon granulated garlic
  ½  teaspoon dried oregano
  ¼  teaspoon ground cumin
  ¼  teaspoon freshly ground black pepper

  4  skinless redfish or red snapper fillets,
     6 to 8 ounces each and about ¾ inch thick
     Extra virgin olive oil

### Salsa

  4  medium plum tomatoes, 3 to 4 ounces each, cored
     and quartered
  ½  cup finely chopped red onion
  ¼  cup lightly packed fresh cilantro leaves and tender
     stems
1-2  medium red Fresno chile(s), stemmed,
     quartered, and seeded
  2  medium garlic cloves, crushed
  1  tablespoon extra virgin olive oil
  1  tablespoon fresh lime juice
  ½  teaspoon pure chile powder
  ¼  teaspoon ground cumin

     Kosher salt
     Freshly ground black pepper

**1.** In a small bowl mix the rub ingredients.

**2.** Lightly coat the fillets with the oil. Season evenly with the rub. Cover and refrigerate.

**3.** Prepare a two-zone fire for high heat (see pages 14-15).

**4.** In a large bowl mix the salsa ingredients. Lay a large sheet of aluminum foil (about 2 feet long) flat on a work surface. Pile the salsa ingredients in the center of the foil. Fold in the edges to create a sealed packet.

**5.** Grill the packet over *direct high heat*, with the lid closed as much as possible, until the tomatoes are soft and the chiles are crisp-tender, about 10 minutes, carefully turning once. Using tongs, remove the packet from the grill and carefully open it so the vegetables don't overcook. Let cool for 5 to 10 minutes. Pour the contents of the packet into a food processor or blender. Pulse just enough to make a chunky salsa. If it seems too wet, drain off some of the juices. Add salt and pepper to taste.

**6.** At this point, to grill the fillets, you may need to add more charcoal to the fire for high heat.

**7.** When the fire is ready, brush the cooking grate clean. Grill the fish fillets over *direct high heat*, with the lid closed as much as possible, until the fish is just beginning to separate into layers and the color is opaque at the center, 6 to 8 minutes, turning once after 4 to 5 minutes. Swap their positions as needed for even cooking. Serve warm with the salsa spooned over the top.

**Makes 4 servings**

Redfish is found in the waters all along the southern Gulf states. It is similar to red snapper but with a slightly firmer, meatier texture. Ling cod also works well for this spicy recipe. Regardless of the type of fish, grill the first side over very hot charcoal for a couple of minutes longer than you grill the second side. This will help you turn the fish without sticking and it will create an even doneness throughout.

# DAVE SCULLY

Dave Scully leads the life of a financial manager, crunching numbers and balancing risks for a hedge fund in New York City. Similar jobs at firms in London, Tokyo, and San Francisco have sent him crisscrossing the globe for decades, but every summer, without fail, Dave returns to a little town on the coast of Maine where the unhurried life isn't much different today than it was when Dave was a boy, or even when Dave's father was a boy. Dave's children are now the fifth generation of Scullys to spend their summers there. "This is where we anchor ourselves," says Dave. "The program is real simple. We dig for clams. We sail and fish a lot, and dinner is usually just a matter of lighting up the kettle and grilling whatever is in season."

During August, striped bass run in the cold waters off Maine's rugged shoreline. Native corn and white peaches are peaking. The corn is so sweet you can

eat it raw, but Dave says that charring it over open flames makes it even tastier. He uses both the corn and the peaches in his own salsa, which he spoons over grilled bass in soft tacos. It's a recipe that captures a particular time and a place. Nothing fancy. Nothing complicated. Just the way summer in Maine should be.

The thickness of your fish fillets, says Dave Scully, determines the type of heat you need to use. If the fillets are an inch or less thick, grill them right over the charcoal, but if they are more than an inch thick, cook them off to the side of the charcoal, so the center of each fillet can cook completely before the outside is overdone. Either way—with direct or indirect heat—grill the fillets with the skin down, and don't turn them. The skin protects the delicate flesh from the fire and holds it together. When the fish are done, scoop the flesh right off the skins with a spatula. If it happens to fall to pieces, no worries. You have to break it apart for the tacos anyway.

Striped bass is done (but still juicy) when the color just turns opaque at the center.

Sliding a spatula between the skin and flesh leaves any charred skin behind on the grate.

# Dave's Fish Tacos

**Prep time: 35 minutes**
**Soaking time for cabbage: 1 hour**
**Grilling time: 14 to 18 minutes**

### Slaw

- 1 small head green cabbage, about 1 pound
  Kosher salt
- 2 tablespoons red wine vinegar
- 1 teaspoon minced garlic
- ½ teaspoon freshly ground black pepper
- ⅓ cup extra virgin olive oil

### Salsa

- 1 large white peach (or nectarine),
  cut into ½-inch chunks
- 2 tablespoons finely chopped fresh mint
- 2 tablespoons finely chopped fresh cilantro
- 1 tablespoon fresh lime juice
- 1 tablespoon minced serrano chile pepper
  Kosher salt
- 2 ears very ripe corn, husked
  Extra virgin olive oil

- 6 striped bass fillets, each about 8 ounces
  and 1 inch thick
- 1 teaspoon kosher salt
- ½ teaspoon freshly ground black pepper
- 12 flour tortillas (8 inches)

**1.** Remove and discard the tough outer leaves from the cabbage. Cut away and discard the triangular core. Slice the cabbage as thinly as you can. You should have about 6 cups. Put the sliced cabbage into a large bowl. Add 1 tablespoon of kosher salt and cover with water. Let stand at room temperature for about 1 hour.

**2.** Drain and dry the cabbage thoroughly in a salad spinner or press between kitchen towels. Put the cabbage into a large bowl. In a small bowl whisk the vinegar, garlic, and pepper with ½ teaspoon kosher salt. Add the olive oil slowly, whisking all the time. Keep whisking until the dressing is opaque. This may take a minute or so. Lightly coat the cabbage with the dressing (you may not need all of it) and toss together. The cabbage can be made up to this point several hours before serving.

**3.** In a medium bowl combine the peach chunks, mint, cilantro, lime juice, chile pepper, and ¼ teaspoon of kosher salt.

**4.** Prepare a two-zone fire for high heat (see pages 14-15).

**5.** Lightly coat the ears of corn with oil. Brush the cooking grate clean. Grill the corn over *direct high heat*, with the lid closed as much as possible, until lightly charred in spots on all sides, 6 to 8 minutes, turning them every couple of minutes. Swap their positions as needed for even cooking. When cool enough to handle, cut off the kernels. Add them to the peach mixture. Season with salt to taste.

**6.** Lightly coat the fish fillets on both sides with oil. Season them on the flesh side with the salt and pepper.

**7.** If the grill is not hot enough, fill a chimney starter about ¼ full with unlit charcoal (20 to 25 briquettes or an equivalent amount of lump charcoal) and spread the unlit charcoal evenly over the lit charcoal. Make sure your bed of charcoal spreads wide enough that you can grill all 6 fillets over direct heat. Leave the lid off so the new charcoal will be fully lit in 10 to 15 minutes. Then put the lid on for about 5 minutes.

**8.** Brush the cooking grate clean. Grill the fish fillets over *direct high heat*, with the lid closed as much as possible, until the flesh is just barely beginning to separate into flakes and the color is opaque in the center, 6 to 8 minutes, without turning (it's okay if the skin burns). Slide a long-handled spatula between the skin and flesh of each fillet and transfer the flesh to a bowl. Break the flesh into bite-size chunks. Now it should be easy to lift the fish skins off the grate with tongs. Brush the cooking grate clean.

**9.** Warm the tortillas, a few at a time, over direct heat, with the lid open, 5 to 10 seconds per side. Fill each tortilla with some fish, some slaw, and some salsa. Serve warm.

**Makes 6 servings**

195

# Veracruz Scallops with Cool Green Chile Sauce

**Prep time: 20 minutes**
**Grilling time: 7 to 11 minutes**

**Sauce**

  3  long Anaheim chile peppers
  3  scallions, root ends discarded,
     all the rest roughly chopped
  ¼  cup lightly packed fresh cilantro leaves
     and tender stems
  1  small garlic clove
  ½  cup sour cream
  ½  cup mayonnaise
     Finely grated zest and juice of 1 lime
  ¼  teaspoon kosher salt

**Rub**

  1  teaspoon pure chile powder
  1  teaspoon paprika
  1  teaspoon kosher salt
  ½  teaspoon ground cumin
  ½  teaspoon dried oregano
  ¼  teaspoon freshly ground black pepper

  24  large scallops, about 1½ ounces each
     Vegetable oil
     Finely grated zest and juice of 1 lime

**1.** Prepare a two-zone fire for high heat (see pages 14-15).

**2.** Brush the cooking grate clean. Grill the chile peppers over ***direct high heat***, with the lid open, until they are blackened and blistered in spots all over, 3 to 5 minutes, turning occasionally. Remove the chiles from the grill. When cool enough to handle, remove and discard the stem ends. Using a sharp knife, scrape off and discard nearly all the blackened skins. Roughly chop the remaining parts of the chiles and drop them into a food processor or blender. Add the scallions, cilantro, and garlic. Process to make a coarse paste, scraping down the sides once or twice. Add the remaining sauce ingredients and process for a minute or two to create a smooth sauce. If it seems too thick, add a little water and adjust the seasonings.

**3.** In a small bowl mix the rub ingredients.

**4.** Rinse the scallops under cold water and remove the small, tough muscle that might be left on each one. Place the scallops in a large bowl and add enough oil to lightly coat them. Add the rub, lime zest, and lime juice. Mix well to coat the scallops evenly.

**5.** At this point, to grill the scallops, you will need to add more charcoal to the fire for high heat. Make sure the bed of charcoal spreads wide enough so that you can grill all 24 scallops over direct heat.

**6.** When the fire is ready, brush the cooking grate clean. Lay the scallops in orderly rows and grill over ***direct high heat***, with the lid closed as much as possible, until slightly firm on the surface and opaque in the center, 4 to 6 minutes, turning once (check one by cutting it open). If you have a nice, even fire, keep the scallops in their original order. If not, you may need to swap their positions for even cooking. Remove them from the grill and serve warm with the sauce.

**Makes 4 to 6 servings**

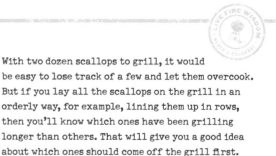

With two dozen scallops to grill, it would be easy to lose track of a few and let them overcook. But if you lay all the scallops on the grill in an orderly way, for example, lining them up in rows, then you'll know which ones have been grilling longer than others. That will give you a good idea about which ones should come off the grill first.

# Greek Seafood Salad

**Prep time: 20 minutes**
**Marinating time: 20 to 30 minutes**
**Grilling time: 3 to 5 minutes**

**Dressing**
¼  cup plus 2 tablespoons extra virgin olive oil
 3  tablespoons red wine vinegar
½  teaspoon minced garlic
½  teaspoon kosher salt
½  teaspoon dried oregano
¼  teaspoon crushed red chile flakes

 5  medium vine-ripened red tomatoes
½  cup pitted green olives, each one halved or quartered
½  cup thinly sliced celery
¼  cup finely diced red onion
 1  pound small shrimp (36-45 count),
    peeled and deveined
 1  pound small bay scallops
 2  tablespoons roughly chopped fresh Italian parsley

**1.** In a small bowl whisk the dressing ingredients.

**2.** Slice the tomatoes crosswise about ½ inch thick and arrange the slices on a serving platter. In a small bowl mix the olives, celery, and onion.

**3.** In a large bowl combine the shrimp and scallops. Add ¼ cup of the dressing and mix well to coat the seafood. Cover and refrigerate for 20 to 30 minutes.

**4.** Prepare a two-zone fire for high heat (see pages 14-15).

**5.** Drain the seafood in a sieve. Spread the seafood in a single layer on a perforated grilling basket and cook over *direct high heat*, with the lid closed as much as possible, until the shrimp and scallops are slightly firm on the surface and completely opaque in the center, 3 to 5 minutes, turning the seafood once or twice for even cooking. With insulated mitts remove the pan from the grill and rest it on a baking sheet. Transfer the seafood to a large bowl to stop the cooking.

Sautéing with the benefit of smoke.

**6.** Spoon the seafood over the tomatoes. Scatter the olives, celery, and onion over the seafood. Spoon some of the dressing over the entire salad (you may not need all of it). Sprinkle the parsley over the top. Serve at room temperature.

**Makes 6 servings**

# Shrimp with Sweet-and-Sour Glaze

**Prep time: 15 minutes**
**Grilling time: 3 to 5 minutes**

**Glaze**
- 1 tablespoon peanut or vegetable oil
- 2 teaspoons minced garlic
- 1 teaspoon grated fresh ginger
- 3 tablespoons orange marmalade
- 2 tablespoons rice vinegar
- 1 teaspoon Dijon mustard
- 1 teaspoon fish sauce

- ½ teaspoon kosher salt
- ½ teaspoon pure chile powder
- ½ teaspoon paprika
- ¼ teaspoon freshly ground black pepper
- 2 pounds extra-large shrimp (16-20 count), peeled and deveined
  Peanut or vegetable oil

**1.** In a small saucepan over medium heat, warm the oil. Add the garlic and ginger and cook until golden brown, 30 to 60 seconds, stirring often. Add the remaining sauce ingredients. Cook until the marmalade has melted, 30 to 60 seconds, stirring often. Remove the saucepan from the heat.

**2.** In a small bowl mix the salt, chile powder, paprika, and pepper. Place the shrimp in a large bowl. Season with the spices. Add just enough oil to lightly coat the shrimp. Mix well. Cover and refrigerate for up to 1 hour.

**3.** Prepare a two-zone fire for high heat (see pages 14-15).

**4.** Brush the cooking grate clean. Grill the shrimp over **_direct high heat_**, with the lid closed as much as possible, until lightly charred on the outside and just turning opaque in the center, 3 to 5 minutes, turning once or twice and swapping their positions as needed for even cooking. Cut open 1 or 2 shrimp to check for doneness.

**5.** Place the cooked shrimp into a large bowl. Spoon some of the glaze over the top (you probably won't need all of it) and mix well. Serve immediately.

**Makes 4 to 6 servings**

# Driftwood-Grilled Lobster Tails

**Prep time: 15 minutes**
**Grilling time: 7 to 11 minutes**

¾ cup (1½ sticks) unsalted butter
3 tablespoons finely chopped fresh chives
4 Maine lobster tails, about 10 ounces each
½ teaspoon sea salt
2 lemons, cut into eighths

8 wooden skewers, soaked in water for
   at least 30 minutes

**1.** Prepare a two-zone fire for high heat (see pages 14-15) or, if you happen to be at the shore, light dried driftwood or charcoal in a hole dug in the sand. Push the driftwood or charcoal to one side of the hole and place a cooking grate on top. *Note: With all the butter in this recipe and the potential for ocean breezes to kick up the flames, be prepared to move the lobster away from the flames.*

**2.** In a small saucepan off to the side of the charcoal, heat the butter until just melted. Add the chives.

**3.** Using a pair of kitchen shears, cut each lobster tail in half lengthwise through the hard top shell and the meat, keeping the shell attached to the meat. Skewer each split tail with a soaked wooden skewer to keep it from curling as it cooks. Brush the lobster meat with some of the chive butter and season with the salt.

**4.** Brush the cooking grate clean. Grill the lobsters, flesh side down, over ***direct high heat***, with the lid off, for about 3 minutes. Turn the lobsters over, brush with more chive butter and continue grilling for 4 to 8 minutes, basting with butter occasionally. Swap their positions as needed for even cooking. When the lobster is done, the shells will be a rich reddish-brown and the meat will be firm, juicy, and coral-white. Squeeze the lemons over the lobster and serve immediately with the remaining butter.

**Makes 4 servings**

# SIDES

# Ember-Roasted Corn with Latino Flavors

**Prep time: 10 minutes**
**Grilling time: 15 to 20 minutes**

**Butter**
¼ cup (½ stick) unsalted butter, softened
2 teaspoons finely chopped fresh oregano
½ teaspoon kosher salt
¼ teaspoon chipotle chile powder
⅛ teaspoon granulated garlic
⅛ teaspoon freshly ground black pepper

4 ears sweet corn (white or yellow), in husks

**1.** Prepare a three-zone split fire for medium heat (see page 17).

**2.** In a small bowl mash the butter ingredients with the back of a fork. Mix until evenly distributed.

**3.** Trim the pointed end of each ear of corn, cutting off and discarding the fine "silk" sticking out of the husk. Remove and discard a layer or two of the tough outer leaves of each husk.

**4.** Carefully lay the ears of corn in a single layer on the charcoal grate, between the coals. Cook the ears of corn there, with the lid closed as much as possible, until the husks are browned and blackened in spots all over and the kernels are tender, 15 to 20 minutes, swapping the positions of the ears and rolling them over a few times for even cooking. If the outer leaves burn, that's okay.

Turn the ears of corn occasionally and swap their positions for even roasting.

**5.** Carefully remove the ears of corn from the grill with long-handled tongs. Use a thick kitchen towel to work with 1 ear of corn at a time. Carefully peel off and discard the husk and silk from each ear of corn. Leave the stem ends attached to use as handles. Smear the butter mixture evenly over the kernels. Serve warm.

**Makes 4 servings**

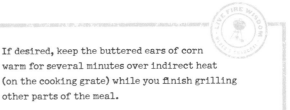

If desired, keep the buttered ears of corn warm for several minutes over indirect heat (on the cooking grate) while you finish grilling other parts of the meal.

# Melted Onions

**Prep time: 10 minutes**
**Grilling time: 1¼ to 1¾ hours**

  6  medium yellow onions (skin on), 8 to 10 ounces each, about the size of a tennis ball
  ¼  cup (½ stick) unsalted butter
  ½  teaspoon kosher salt
  ¼  teaspoon freshly ground black pepper
  1  teaspoon sherry vinegar
  1  tablespoon minced fresh Italian parsley

**1.** Prepare a two-zone fire for medium heat (see pages 14-15).

**2.** With the onions still in their skins, place them on the charcoal grate against the charcoal. Close the lid and cook the onions until very tender, 1 to 1½ hours. Occasionally swap the positions of the onions for even cooking and turn the blackened skins away from the charcoal. When very tender, the onions will be blackened in spots all over and a knife blade will slide in and out of each onion like it is a ripe peach. Some onions may take longer than others.

**3.** At this point, to finish cooking the onions, you will need to add more charcoal to the fire for medium heat.

**4.** Remove the onions from the grill and let cool completely. Carefully remove the skin from each onion, being careful to leave the root ends intact so they hold the layers of the onions together. Cut each onion lengthwise through the stem and root ends.

As the charcoal singes the onion skins, it sweetens and melts what's inside.

**5.** When the fire is ready, put the cooking grate in place. In a 9 x 13-inch, heavy-duty foil pan over **_direct medium heat_**, melt the butter. Carefully add the onions in a single layer and season with the salt and pepper. Using tongs, turn the onions in the butter to coat them.

**6.** Slide the pan over **_indirect medium heat_** and cook, with the lid closed as much as possible, until the onions are very tender and just beginning to brown, 10 to 15 minutes, carefully turning the onions once or twice. If desired, to keep the onions warm, cover the pan with foil and let the onions continue to cook over indirect heat for as long as 30 minutes. Using insulated mitts, remove the pan from the grill. Splash the vinegar and sprinkle the parsley over the onions. Serve warm.

**Makes 4 to 6 servings**

# Grilled Artichoke Hearts

**Prep time: 30 minutes**
**Grilling time: 4 to 6 minutes**

    6  large artichokes, 10 to 12 ounces each
       Juice of 1 lemon
    2  tablespoons extra virgin olive oil
    ½  teaspoon kosher salt

**1.** Bring a large pot (8 to 10 quarts) of salted water to a boil.

**2.** Trim the stem of each artichoke, leaving about 1 inch attached. Snap off the dark outer leaves until you expose the yellowish leaves with pale green tips. Lay each artichoke on its side and cut off the remaining leaves just above the base. Cut the base of each artichoke in half lengthwise, through the stem, and drop each half into a large bowl of water mixed with the lemon juice.

**3.** One at a time, lift each artichoke from the lemon water and use a teaspoon to scoop out the purplish leaves and fuzzy "choke." Then use a small, sharp knife to trim and smooth the rough and greenish areas around the base. Trim the tough outer layer of the stem. After each artichoke heart is trimmed, return it to the lemon water.

**4.** Drain the artichoke hearts and cook them in the boiling salted water until you can pierce them easily with a knife, 10 to 12 minutes, but don't overcook them. Drain the artichokes in a colander and place them in a large bowl.

While still warm, add the oil and salt. Toss gently to coat the artichokes. *Note: The artichokes may be made up to this point and refrigerated for up to 4 hours. Bring to room temperature before grilling.*

**5.** Prepare a two-zone fire for medium heat (see pages 14-15).

**6.** Lift the artichoke hearts from the bowl and let any excess oil drip back into the bowl. Brush the cooking grate clean. Grill the artichokes over ***direct medium heat***, with the lid closed as much as possible, until warm and lightly charred, 4 to 6 minutes, turning them once or twice and swapping their positions as needed for even cooking. If desired, baste them on the grill once or twice with the oil remaining in the bowl. Serve warm.

**Makes 6 servings**

An artichoke in 3 stages: whole, without its tough leaves, and just the heart (with some tender stem attached).

# Grilled Asparagus with Balsamic Syrup

**Prep time: 5 minutes**
**Grilling time: 4 to 6 minutes**

½ cup inexpensive balsamic vinegar
2 pounds medium asparagus (40 to 50 spears),
  each about ½ inch thick at the stem end
¼ cup extra virgin olive oil
½ teaspoon kosher salt
¼ teaspoon freshly ground black pepper

**1.** Prepare a two-zone fire for medium heat (see pages 14-15).

**2.** If you plan to do this next step on an indoor stove, turn on the fan in the stove's hood. The simmering vinegar creates a pungent aroma. In a small saucepan bring the vinegar to a simmer over medium heat, then reduce the heat until a few bubbles are just breaking through the surface. Cook at a slow simmer until about ¼ cup of vinegar remains. As you get close to ¼ cup, the vinegar will cling to the back of a spoon and it will coat the bottom of the saucepan when you rock it back and forth. The total cooking time will be roughly 10 minutes, but keep an eye on the vinegar. If it cooks too quickly or it reduces too much, it will turn bitter rather than sweet. Remove the saucepan from the heat and let cool to room temperature (the syrup will continue to thicken as it cools).

**3.** Remove and discard any tough, woody ends from the asparagus spears. Peel the ends of the asparagus, if desired. Lightly coat the asparagus with the oil. Season evenly with the salt and pepper. Brush the cooking grate clean. Lay the asparagus perpendicular to the bars on the cooking grate. Grill over **_direct medium heat_**, with the lid closed as much as possible, until lightly charred and crisp-tender, 4 to 6 minutes, rolling the spears a couple times and swapping their positions as needed for even cooking.

**4.** Arrange the asparagus on a platter or individual plates. If the syrup is stiff, warm it briefly over medium heat. Drizzle some of the syrup over the spears (you may not need all of it). Season with more salt, if desired. Serve warm or at room temperature.

**Makes 6 servings**

As if balsamic vinegar isn't deeply flavored enough, when you cook it down very slowly, it turns to a sweet-and-sour syrup that adds a lot of jazz to grilled asparagus. Remember, though, balsamic syrup is a potent potion. Use it very sparingly.

# Twice-Cooked Potatoes with Wasabi

**Prep time: 10 minutes**
**Grilling time: 40 to 50 minutes**

  4  russet potatoes, 8 to 10 ounces each, washed and
      halved lengthwise
      Vegetable oil
  ¾  cup sour cream
1½  cups shredded Monterey Jack cheese,
      about 3 ounces, divided
  2  teaspoons Dijon mustard
  1  teaspoon wasabi paste
  1  teaspoon kosher salt
  ¼  teaspoon freshly ground black pepper

**1.** Prepare a two-zone fire for medium heat (see pages 14-15).

**2.** Lightly coat the potato halves with oil. Brush the cooking grate clean. Grill the potatoes over ***direct medium heat***, with the lid closed as much as possible, until a fork slides in and out easily, 30 to 40 minutes, turning 3 or 4 times and swapping their positions as needed for even cooking. If the potatoes begin to turn darker than golden brown, finish cooking them over indirect heat. Remove the potatoes from the grill and let cool slightly.

**3.** When cool enough to handle, use a small, sharp knife or the edge of a spoon to cut around the cut side of the potato to within ¼ inch of the skin. Scrape off and discard any charred sections of potato. Using a spoon, scoop out the interior of the potato, leaving a shell about ¼ inch thick attached to the skin. Place the potato pulp in a large bowl. Set the potato shells aside while preparing the stuffing.

**4.** Using a potato masher or the back of a fork, mash the potato pulp in the bowl. Add the sour cream and mix well. Stir in half of the cheese and all of the remaining ingredients. Taste the potato mixture and, if desired, add more wasabi, salt, and pepper to taste. Spoon the potato mixture into the shells, mounding it slightly. Sprinkle the remaining cheese over the tops of the potatoes.

**5.** At this point, to finish the potatoes, you may need to add more charcoal to the fire for medium heat. When the fire is ready, grill the stuffed potatoes over ***indirect medium heat***, with the lid closed as much as possible, until the cheese is melted and the potatoes are heated through, 10 to 15 minutes. Serve immediately.

**Makes 4 to 8 servings**

# Grilled Carrots

**Prep time: 10 minutes**
**Grilling time: 3 to 5 minutes**

>  8  medium carrots, each 6 to 8 inches long and
>     about 1 inch wide at the stem
>  ¼  cup unsalted butter
>  ½  teaspoon red wine vinegar
>  ¼  teaspoon freshly ground nutmeg
>  ½  teaspoon kosher salt, divided
>  ¼  teaspoon freshly ground black pepper, divided
>  1  teaspoon minced fresh Italian parsley

**1.** Peel the carrots and cook them in boiling water until they are partially cooked but still crisp, 4 to 6 minutes. Drain the carrots and rinse them under cold water for at least 10 seconds to stop the cooking.

**2.** Prepare a two-zone fire for high heat (see pages 14-15).

**3.** Lay the carrots flat on a work surface. In a small saucepan over medium heat, melt the butter with the vinegar and nutmeg. Brush the carrots with about half the butter mixture and season with half the salt and pepper.

**4.** Brush the cooking grate clean. Grill the carrots over **direct high heat**, with the lid open, until lightly charred with spots and stripes, 3 to 5 minutes, turning occasionally and swapping their positions as needed for even cooking. Move the carrots to a platter, brush them with the remaining butter mixture, and season them with the remaining salt and pepper. Sprinkle the parsley over the top. Serve warm.

**Makes 4 servings**

> I first saw grilled carrots on the menu of a Hollywood restaurant called Dominick's. Basted with butter and caramelized over split logs of white oak, they were superb. I have added a little vinegar to balance the natural sweetness of the carrots and some fresh parsley to finish the dish.

# Acorn Squash with Brown Butter and Garlic

**Prep time: 10 minutes**
**Grilling time: 40 to 60 minutes**

**Glaze**
>  3  tablespoons unsalted butter, cut into 3 equal pieces
>  2  tablespoons dark brown sugar
>  2  teaspoons minced garlic
>  1  teaspoon kosher salt
>  ¼  teaspoon freshly ground black pepper
>  ¼  teaspoon freshly grated nutmeg
>  1  tablespoon cider vinegar
>
>  2  small acorn squashes, each about 1½ pounds,
>     the size of a softball

**1.** In a small saucepan or skillet combine all the glaze ingredients except the vinegar. Cook over medium-high heat for 2 to 3 minutes, stirring occasionally. Remove from the heat and let cool to room temperature.

**2.** Prepare a two-zone fire for high heat (see pages 14-15).

**3.** With a large knife, carefully cut the squashes in half lengthwise. Scoop out and discard the seeds and strings. Add the vinegar to the cooled glaze. Brush the glaze over the exposed flesh of the squashes.

**4.** Brush the cooking grate clean. Grill the squashes, with the exposed flesh facing up, over **indirect high heat**, with the lid closed as much as possible, until the exposed flesh browns on the surface and a sharp knife inserted all the way into the flesh slides out very easily, 40 to 60 minutes, basting occasionally with the glaze that pools in the bowl of the squashes. For even cooking, you may need to swap the positions of the squashes. If any of the squashes are browning too quickly or you wish to slow down the cooking, move them farther from the charcoal. When the squashes are fully cooked and tender, remove them from the grill and serve warm.

**Makes 4 servings**

Grilled Carrots

Acorn Squash with Brown Butter and Garlic

211

# Bacon, Lettuce, and Grilled Tomato Salad

**Prep time: 20 minutes**
**Grilling time: 6 to 7 minutes**

½  pound thick-sliced bacon, cut into bite-size pieces
   Extra virgin olive oil
2  tablespoons minced shallot
1½  tablespoons sherry vinegar
1  teaspoon finely chopped fresh thyme
¼  teaspoon kosher salt
⅛  teaspoon freshly ground black pepper
1½  pints cherry tomatoes, stemmed
1  large, crusty sandwich roll, cut in half lengthwise
1-2  medium heads butter lettuce
2-3  scallions, white and light green parts, thinly sliced

**1.** Prepare a two-zone fire for medium heat (see pages 14-15).

**2.** In a large skillet over medium heat, cook the bacon until crisp. With a slotted spoon, transfer the bacon to paper towels, reserving the bacon fat. Add enough olive oil to the bacon fat to make 6 tablespoons.

**3.** In a small bowl mix the shallot, vinegar, thyme, salt, and pepper. Whisk in the bacon fat/oil mixture in a steady stream to make a dressing.

**4.** Lightly coat the tomatoes with some of the dressing. Grill the tomatoes in a vegetable basket over *direct medium heat*, with the lid closed as much as possible, until their skins begin to char and crack, 5 to 6 minutes, shaking the basket with an insulated mitt to turn them. Using the insulated mitt, carefully remove the vegetable basket from the grill and pour the tomatoes into a bowl.

A perforated basket prevents small tomatoes from falling through the grate.

**5.** Brush the cut side of the roll with some of the dressing and grill over *direct medium heat*, with the lid open, until toasted, about 1 minute, without turning. Remove from the grill and cut into large croutons.

**6.** Arrange the lettuce leaves in a serving bowl. Add the tomatoes with their juices, as well as the croutons, among the lettuce leaves. Whisk the dressing one more time and spoon some over the salad (you may not need all of it). Top with the bacon and finish with the scallions. Serve right away at room temperature.

**Makes 4 servings**

# Fennel, Pepper, and Mozzarella Salad

**Prep time: 15 minutes**
**Grilling time: 20 to 25 minutes**

## Dressing

  3  tablespoons extra virgin olive oil
  1  tablespoon red wine vinegar
  1  teaspoon minced garlic
  ¾  teaspoon anchovy paste
  ¼  teaspoon crushed red chile flakes
  ¼  teaspoon kosher salt

## Salad

  2  medium fennel bulbs, 8 to 10 ounces each, stalks and fronds removed, with the root ends intact
  2  roasted red bell peppers, cut into ½-inch dice
  ½  pound fresh mozzarella, cut into ½-inch dice
  ½  cup pitted black olives, rinsed, and roughly chopped
  3  tablespoons roughly chopped fresh basil

    Kosher salt
    Freshly ground black pepper

1. In a small bowl whisk the dressing ingredients.

2. Cut each fennel bulb in half lengthwise, through the stem, into 2 wide, flat halves. Lightly brush the bulbs on all sides with some of the dressing.

3. In a large bowl combine the remaining salad ingredients.

4. Prepare a two-zone fire for medium heat (see pages 14-15).

5. Brush the cooking grate clean. Grill the fennel halves, cut sides down, over ***direct medium heat***, with the lid closed as much as possible, until lightly charred but not burned, 5 to 7 minutes, swapping their positions as needed for even cooking. Turn the fennel over and grill for another 3 minutes, then move them over indirect heat. Cook over ***indirect medium heat***, with the lid closed as much as possible, until crisp-tender when pierced with the tip of a knife, 12 to 15 minutes, swapping their positions as needed for even cooking. Remove the fennel from the grill and let cool.

6. When cool enough to handle, cut away and discard the hard, triangular core of each half. Cut the remaining fennel into ½-inch pieces. Add them to the bowl with the salad ingredients. Add as much of the remaining dressing as you like to moisten the salad. Mix well. Season with salt and pepper to taste. Serve at room temperature.

**Makes 6 servings**

# Roasted Eggplant and Tomato Salad

**Prep time: 20 minutes**
**Grilling time: 15 to 20 minutes**

### Dressing

   3  tablespoons extra virgin olive oil
   2  tablespoons fresh lemon juice
  ½  tablespoon finely grated ginger
  ½  teaspoon minced garlic
  ½  teaspoon ground cumin
  ½  teaspoon kosher salt
  ⅛  teaspoon ground cayenne pepper

1½  cups seeded, ½-inch-diced tomatoes
  ½  teaspoon kosher salt
  2  medium globe eggplants, about 1 pound each
  ¼  cup thinly sliced scallions
  ¼  cup roughly chopped fresh cilantro or parsley

**1.** In a small bowl whisk the dressing ingredients. Let stand at room temperature for about 30 minutes.

**2.** In a small bowl toss the tomatoes with the salt. Set aside for 15 to 30 minutes to bring out their juices. Then drain the tomatoes and place them in a large serving bowl.

**3.** Prepare a two-zone fire for high heat (see pages 14-15).

**4.** Prick the eggplants several times with a fork. Brush the cooking grate clean. Grill the eggplants over **_direct high heat_**, with the lid closed as much as possible, until the skins are charred and the eggplants begin to

When the eggplant is fully cooked, the skin will crack and the shape will collapse.

collapse, 15 to 20 minutes, turning occasionally. A knife should slide in and out of the flesh without resistance. Set the eggplants aside on a plate until cool enough to handle.

**5.** Cut the eggplants in half lengthwise and, with a large spoon, scrape the flesh away from the skin. Discard the skin and any large seed pockets in the flesh. Roughly chop the flesh of the eggplants.

**6.** Combine the chopped eggplant and scallions with the tomatoes. Mix gently. Add as much of the dressing as you like to moisten and flavor the salad (you may not need all of it). Sprinkle the cilantro or parsley over the top just before serving. Serve at room temperature.

**Makes 4 to 6 servings**

In India, where this dish originated, coconut shells burn to high-heat embers and subtle smokiness, a good combination for roasting vegetables.

# Grilled Vegetable and Orzo Salad

**Prep time: 20 minutes**
**Grilling time: 12 to 15 minutes**

½ pound orzo pasta
6 tablespoons extra virgin olive oil
2 tablespoons balsamic vinegar
2 teaspoons minced garlic
2 teaspoons Dijon mustard
1 teaspoon kosher salt
1 teaspoon freshly ground black pepper
2 ears yellow corn, husked
2 medium zucchini, halved lengthwise
1 medium red bell pepper, quartered and seeded
1 cup grape tomatoes or small cherry tomatoes
4 ounces crumbled feta cheese
¼ cup roughly chopped fresh Italian parsley or basil

**1.** Prepare a two-zone fire for medium heat (see pages 14-15).

**2.** Cook the orzo according to the package directions. Drain and set aside in a large bowl.

**3.** In a small bowl whisk the olive oil, vinegar, garlic, mustard, salt, and pepper until smooth. Lightly coat the corn, zucchini, and bell pepper with about half of the olive oil mixture. Reserve the rest for dressing the salad.

**4.** Brush the cooking grate clean. Grill the vegetables over **direct medium heat**, with the lid closed as much as possible, until lightly charred and crisp-tender, turning and swapping their positions as needed for even cooking. The corn will take 12 to 15 minutes. It should be golden brown in spots all over. The zucchini will take 4 to 6 minutes. While the surface should be lightly charred, the centers should be slightly firm. The pepper will take 4 to 6 minutes. They can burn quickly so turn them as needed. After they cool, scrape off any burnt pieces.

**5.** When the corn is cool enough to handle, slice the kernels into the bowl of orzo. Use the back of the knife to scrape the milky yellow corn juice from the cobs. Then discard the cobs. Cut the zucchini and pepper crosswise into ½-inch pieces and add them to the bowl. Cut each tomato in half or quarters and add to the bowl along with the cheese and parsley. Add as much of the remaining dressing as you like to moisten and flavor the salad (you may not need all of it). Season with salt and pepper to taste. Serve at room temperature.

**Makes about 8 cups**

This recipe calls for cutting zucchini lengthwise into halves instead of thin planks. The bigger, thicker pieces remain slightly firm in the center even after you lightly char their surfaces, which means a better texture for this salad.

# Mac and Cheese with Poblano Chiles and Scallions

**Prep time: 30 minutes**
**Grilling time: 33 to 40 minutes**

3-4 medium poblano chile peppers, about ¾ pound total
½ pound baked ham, sliced about ⅓ inch thick
6 scallions, including the green tops
    Extra virgin olive oil
4 tablespoons unsalted butter, plus a little extra
    for buttering the baking dish
4 tablespoons all-purpose flour
1 quart whole milk
4 cups (about 12 ounces) shredded
    Monterey Jack cheese, divided
¼ cup grated Parmigiano-Reggiano cheese
¾ teaspoon kosher salt
¼ teaspoon freshly ground black pepper
10 ounces large elbow macaroni
½ cup fresh bread crumbs
2 teaspoons finely chopped fresh thyme

**1.** Prepare a three-zone split fire for medium heat (see page 17).

**2.** Lightly coat the chiles, sliced ham, and scallions with oil. Brush the cooking grate clean. Grill the chiles over **direct medium heat**, with the lid closed as much as possible, until evenly charred on all sides, 8 to 10 minutes, turning as needed. At the same time, grill the ham and scallions over **direct medium heat** until lightly charred, 4 to 5 minutes, turning once or twice and swapping their positions as needed for even cooking. Remove the chiles, ham, and scallions from the grill and let cool. Peel away the charred skins from the chiles. Remove and discard the stems and seeds. Roughly chop the chiles. Dice the ham into ⅓-inch cubes. Thinly slice the scallions crosswise and discard the root ends.

**3.** In a large saucepan over medium heat, melt the butter. As it starts to sizzle, whisk the flour into the butter to form a paste. Cook this mixture until it starts to brown, 3 to 4 minutes, stirring occasionally. Add the milk while whisking to keep lumps from forming. Raise the heat to medium-high. Gradually add 3 cups of the Monterey Jack cheese, all the Parmigiano-Reggiano cheese, the salt, and the pepper. As the cheese melts into the sauce and it begins to boil, lower the heat to a simmer. Cook for 4 to 5 minutes. Remove the cheese sauce from the heat and pour into a buttered 2½- to 3-quart baking dish.

**4.** Cook the macaroni in salted boiling water for 3 minutes less than the cooking time recommended on the package. Drain the macaroni and add it to the baking dish, mixing it with the cheese sauce. Add the chiles, ham, and scallions. Mix well.

**5.** In a small bowl mix the bread crumbs with the remaining 1 cup of Monterey Jack cheese and the thyme. Top the pasta with the bread crumb mixture and gently press it into the surface.

**6.** At this point you may need to add more charcoal to the fire for medium heat.

**7.** When the fire is ready, place the baking dish in the center of the cooking grate and cook over **indirect medium heat**, with the lid closed as much as possible, until the mac and cheese is golden brown on top, 25 to 30 minutes and rotating the dish as needed for even cooking. Using insulated mitts, remove the dish from the grill and let cool slightly. Serve warm.

**Makes 6 to 8 servings**

# PETE MARCZYK

On annual hunting trips into the Colorado Rockies, gourmet grocer Pete Marczyk cooks this cheesy cornbread with a bit of jalapeño heat after he and his buddies have bagged their first elk. He serves the cornbread alongside elk tenderloin, which he coats with bacon fat and wild herbs before grilling it over glowing coals. This ritualized meal is the epitome of rugged campfire cooking and it is also consistent with his priority for "traceability" in food. He likes to know the origin of what he eats and the path it took to his plate (the less processing required the better). For example, notice that he uses a cornbread mix made by Bob's Red Mill, an environmentally conscious company from Oregon that has managed to survive and thrive for decades because of the natural integrity of its whole-grain ingredients and the old millstones it uses to grind them.

Marczyk says, "I'm just not interested in eating food that has been mass-produced and commoditized to the point that it has lost its inherent qualities. I think all natural foods made by hand just taste better." He maintains his preference for natural in charcoal, too. Marczyk grills over lump mesquite coals made in Mexico from fallen branches that otherwise would serve no real purpose.

During the summer Pete Marczyk and his brother, Paul, host "Friday Burger Nights" in the parking lot of their Denver store, Marczyk's Fine Foods. They make their hamburgers from all natural, hormone-free beef and they grill them over pure mesquite charcoal. "Obviously it would be easier for us to use a gas grill or those little briquettes, but that's just not who we are."

The trick to this cornbread is building a good, even fire to one side of the grill and rotating the skillet periodically over indirect heat so that all sections of the cornbread get the right amount of time facing the coals. Pete Marczyk says it takes some practice, and even after years of cooking this, he sometimes waits too long to rotate the skillet, but then again, some slightly burnt, crispy edges do have a certain appeal.

# Pete's Hunting Trip Cornbread

**Prep time: 10 minutes**
**Grilling time: 20 to 30 minutes**

*Note: This recipe calls for a big skillet. Measure 12 inches across the diameter of the bottom of the skillet.*

2½  cups whole milk
  2  large eggs
 ½  cup (1 stick) unsalted butter
  5  cups Bob's Red Mill® cornbread and muffin mix
1½  cups grated cheddar cheese
  1  jalapeño chile pepper, finely grated
  1  teaspoon kosher salt

1. Prepare a two-zone fire for medium heat (see pages 14-15). Push the charcoal all the way to one side so it doesn't cover more than one-third of the charcoal grate.

2. In a large bowl mix the milk and eggs until the eggs are evenly incorporated. Cut the butter into 4 to 6 pieces.

3. Place a 12-inch, cast-iron skillet on the cooking grate but not directly over the charcoal. Melt the butter in the skillet. When the butter is melted (not browned), use an insulated mitt to lift the skillet and pour the butter into the bowl with the milk and eggs. Leave a thin film of butter on the bottom of the skillet to prevent the cornbread from sticking. Put the skillet back on the cooking grate, over *indirect medium heat*, and close the lid while you finish the batter.

4. Add all the remaining ingredients to the bowl and mix gently with a large spoon until evenly distributed. Carefully pour the batter into the hot skillet and spread it out evenly. Close the lid and cook the cornbread over *indirect medium heat* for 20 minutes. Every 5 minutes or so, use an insulated mitt to rotate the skillet a quarter turn so that no one section of the cornbread faces the hot charcoal for too long. Check for doneness after 20 minutes. If a knife inserted into the center comes out wet, close the lid and continue to cook for 5 to 10 minutes more. When done, the cornbread should be golden brown around the top edges and a knife blade inserted into the middle should be a little moist but not wet. Using insulated mitts, remove the skillet from the grill and let the cornbread cool completely in the skillet. Cut into wedges right in the skillet. Serve at room temperature.

**Make 8 to 10 generous servings**

# DESSERTS

# Red Velvet Cake

**Prep time: 45 minutes**
**Baking time: 25 to 35 minutes**

1½  cups granulated sugar
½  cup shortening
2½  cups all-purpose flour
1  teaspoon baking soda
1  teaspoon salt
1  teaspoon cocoa powder
1  cup buttermilk
2  large eggs
2  tablespoons red food coloring
1  teaspoon pure vanilla extract
1  teaspoon white distilled vinegar

**Frosting**
1  box (16 ounces) confectioners' sugar
1  package (8 ounces) cream cheese, softened
1  cup (2 sticks) unsalted butter, softened
1  teaspoon pure vanilla extract

**1.** Preheat the oven to 350°F. Lightly grease and flour two 9-inch cake pans.

**2.** In the bowl of a stand mixer with a paddle attachment, cream the sugar and shortening until light and fluffy, scraping down the sides of the bowl occasionally.

**3.** In a large bowl sift the flour, baking soda, salt, and cocoa powder.

**4.** In another large bowl whisk the buttermilk, eggs, food coloring, vanilla, and vinegar.

**5.** With the stand mixer running on low, add the buttermilk mixture and flour mixture in batches, starting and ending with the buttermilk mixture. Mix just until the batter is smooth.

**6.** Divide the batter evenly among the greased and floured cake pans. Bake on separate oven racks until a toothpick or knife blade inserted into the center comes out clean, 25 to 35 minutes. Halfway through the baking time, swap the position of each pan. When fully cooked, remove the pans from the oven and run a knife along the edges to free the cakes from the pans. Carefully invert the cakes and let them cool completely on racks.

**7.** In a clean bowl of a stand mixer with a paddle attachment, mix the sugar, cream cheese, and butter on low speed until thoroughly combined. Raise the speed to high and mix until the frosting is light and fluffy, then add the vanilla. Occasionally turn off the machine and scrape down the sides of the bowl.

**8.** Put one of the cake layers on a serving platter. Spread the frosting about ½ inch thick. Place the second layer on top. Scoop the remaining frosting out of the bowl and spread it over the top. Continue to spread it to the edges and down the sides of the cake. Serve at room temperature.

**Makes 6 to 8 servings**

Who knows exactly when and where this stunning cake made its debut? One popular story, which is probably wrong, tells of a woman in the 1940s who first tasted it at The Waldorf=Astoria® hotel in New York City. The cake made such an impression that she later wrote to the chef for the recipe, which he provided, along with a bill for $350. Irate and insulted, she swore to get even by giving away the recipe to as many people as possible. One way or another, the recipe made its way to the South and earned a place next to other beloved regional traditions, like ribs and slaw. To this day, many of the best barbecue restaurants keep it on their menus.

# Cherry-Berry Cobbler

**Prep time: 15 minutes**
**Grilling time: 40 to 60 minutes**

½ cup granulated sugar, divided
1 tablespoon cornstarch
1 bag (12 ounces) frozen, pitted, dark sweet cherries, partially thawed, or 2 cups fresh, pitted cherries
1 bag (12 ounces) frozen unsweetened raspberries, partially thawed, or 2 to 3 cups fresh raspberries
½ cup all-purpose flour
½ teaspoon baking powder
¼ teaspoon salt
½ cup (1 stick) unsalted butter, cold, cut into ½-inch dice
1 large egg, beaten
1 pint vanilla ice cream

**1.** Using charcoal briquettes, prepare a three-zone split fire for medium heat (see page 17).

**2.** In a large bowl mix 5 tablespoons of the sugar with the cornstarch. Add the fruit and any thawed juices and gently fold to blend. Spoon into a 9 x 13-inch, heavy-duty foil pan.

**3.** In a food processor pulse the flour, baking powder, salt, and the remaining 3 tablespoons of sugar. Add the butter and pulse a few times to cut the dice into smaller pieces and coat them with the flour mixture. Add the egg and pulse just once or twice to incorporate. With a spoon, place 6 evenly spaced mounds of batter on the surface of the fruit.

**4.** Place the pan on the cooking grate. Make sure there is no charcoal directly below the pan. Cook the cobbler over *indirect medium heat*, with the lid closed as much as possible, until the fruit is bubbly and the topping is golden, 40 to 60 minutes, rotating the pan for even cooking.

**5.** Carefully remove the pan from the grill and let cool at room temperature for 20 to 30 minutes. Serve warm with ice cream.

**Makes 6 to 8 servings**

---

# Caramelized Peaches with Lemon and Blueberries

**Prep time: 10 minutes**
**Grilling time: 8 to 12 minutes**

4 large peaches, firm but ripe, halved and pitted
3 tablespoons unsalted butter, cut into small pieces
2 tablespoons dark brown sugar
½ teaspoon pure vanilla extract
6 tablespoons store-bought lemon curd
2-4 tablespoons heavy cream
1½ cups fresh blueberries

**1.** Using charcoal briquettes, prepare a two-zone fire for medium heat (see pages 14-15).

**2.** Arrange the peaches in a single layer, cut sides down, in a 9 x 13-inch, heavy-duty foil pan. Scatter the butter pieces and sugar between the peaches. Add the vanilla to the pan.

**3.** In a small bowl whisk the lemon curd with enough heavy cream to create a smooth, spoonable sauce.

**4.** Place the pan of peaches over *direct medium heat* and cook, with the lid closed as much as possible, until the peaches are tender, warm, and glazed, 8 to 12 minutes (depending on the size and firmness of the peaches), rolling the peaches gently in the butter mixture once. To keep the peaches warm, slide the pan over indirect heat and remove the grill's lid. When ready to serve, slide the hot pan onto a baking sheet and move to a work surface.

**5.** Cut the peaches into quarters or smaller slices. Arrange in bowls with the blueberries. Serve warm with the lemon curd spooned over the top.

**Makes 4 to 6 servings**

After the peaches have oozed their golden, bubbling juices over direct heat, feel free to slide the pan off to the side of the charcoal and remove the grill's lid. This warm dessert will wait for you there while you finish your main course.

Cherry Berry Cobbler

Caramelized Peaches with Lemon and Blueberries

# Butter-Rum Pineapple with Coconut Ice Cream

**Prep time: 20 minutes**
**Grilling time: 4 to 6 minutes**

  3  tablespoons unsalted butter
  3  tablespoons rum
  1  tablespoon honey
  ⅛  teaspoon ground cinnamon
  6  cored slices of ripe pineapple, each about ⅓ inch thick
  1  pint coconut ice cream or frozen yogurt
  6  ginger crisp cookies, optional
  6  mint sprigs, optional

**1.** Using charcoal briquettes, prepare a two-zone fire for medium heat (see pages 14-15).

**2.** In a small saucepan over low heat, melt the butter with the rum, honey, and cinnamon. Lightly brush the pineapple slices on both sides with some of the butter mixture. Reserve the rest for basting.

**3.** Brush the cooking grate clean. Grill the pineapple slices over ***direct medium heat***, with the lid open, until well marked on both sides, 4 to 6 minutes, turning occasionally and basting with the reserved butter mixture. Swap their positions as needed for even cooking. Transfer the pineapple slices to a cutting board and cut into bite-size pieces.

**4.** Scoop the ice cream into bowls and top with the pineapple. If desired, garnish each bowl with a ginger crisp and a mint sprig.

**Makes 6 servings**

# Roasted Apples on the Half Shell

**Prep time: 15 minutes**
**Grilling time: 30 to 45 minutes**

> 4 ripe, firm-fleshed apples (Jonagold, Braeburn, or Rome), about 8 ounces each
> 1 lemon

**Filling**
> ¼ cup apricot jam
> ¼ cup golden raisins
> 1 tablespoon brandy or rum
> ¼ teaspoon ground allspice
>
> 4 teaspoons unsalted butter
> Heavy cream or vanilla ice cream

**1.** Using charcoal briquettes, prepare a three-zone split fire for medium heat (see page 17).

**2.** Using a small melon baller or grapefruit spoon, remove the stem and scoop out the core of each apple, but do not cut all the way through the bottom. With a vegetable peeler, start at the top of each apple and remove the skin about halfway down, stopping at the equator.

**3.** Cut the lemon in half and rub the cut sides over the exposed apple to prevent it from turning brown.

**4.** In a small bowl combine the filling ingredients. Place each apple on a 12-inch square of heavy-duty aluminum foil and pack each cavity with the filling. Dot each apple with 1 teaspoon of butter. Fold up the sides of the foil to completely wrap each apple.

**5.** Grill the apples over ***indirect medium heat***, with the lid closed as much as possible, until tender when pierced with a knife, 30 to 45 minutes. Remove the apples from the grill and allow to cool in the foil for 5 to 10 minutes. Peel back the foil (or place the apples in individual serving dishes with the reserved juice from the foil packet) and serve warm with heavy cream or ice cream.

**Makes 4 servings**

# Caramelized Plum Upside-Down Cake

**Prep time: 25 minutes**
**Grilling time: 40 to 45 minutes**

  1  cup cake flour (or 2 tablespoons cornstarch
      plus enough all-purpose flour to equal 1 cup)
  1  teaspoon baking powder
  ¼  teaspoon salt
  ⅔  cup granulated sugar
  ½  cup (1 stick) plus 1 tablespoon unsalted butter,
      cut into ¼-inch pieces, softened
  1  large egg
  1  teaspoon pure vanilla extract
  ⅓  cup whole milk
  ¼  cup lightly packed light brown sugar
  3  large plums, firm but ripe, about 1 pound, halved,
      pitted, and each half cut into quarters
  1  cup heavy cream, cold, whipped to stiff peaks

**1.** In a medium bowl mix the flour, baking powder, and salt.

**2.** In the bowl of a stand mixer, cream the sugar with ½ cup of the butter on high speed until light and fluffy, scraping down the sides of the bowl occasionally.

**3.** Add the egg and vanilla and beat until well blended. On low speed, gradually beat in the flour mixture, alternating it with the milk, just until blended.

**4.** Using charcoal briquettes, prepare a three-zone split fire for medium heat (see page 17). Leave a space between the piles large enough for a 9-inch round cake pan.

**5.** Smear the remaining 1 tablespoon of butter in a 9-inch, heavy-duty, round cake pan (or use two disposable foil cake pans, one inside the other) and sprinkle the brown sugar over the butter.

**6.** Arrange the plums on their sides in tight concentric circles on top of the butter and sugar. Spoon the prepared batter evenly on top of the plums and smooth with the back of a spoon.

**7.** Place the cake in the center of the cooking grate and cook over *indirect medium heat*, with the lid closed as much as possible, until the edges pull away from the pan and a skewer inserted in the center comes out clean, 40 to 45 minutes.

**8.** Cool the cake in the pan for 15 minutes before inverting it onto a serving plate. Serve at room temperature with whipped cream.

**Makes 8 servings**

# Grilled Apricots with Pound Cake and Toasted Almonds

**Prep time: 15 minutes**
**Grilling time: 4 to 6 minutes**

**Topping**
- ½ cup heavy cream, cold
- 1 tablespoon granulated sugar
- 1 teaspoon grated orange zest

- 12 medium apricots, firm but ripe
- 6 tablespoons unsalted butter
- 3 tablespoons granulated sugar
- ¼ teaspoon pure almond extract
- 6 slices pound cake, each about ½ inch thick
- Confectioners' sugar
- ⅓ cup toasted sliced almonds

**1.** Using charcoal briquettes, prepare a two-zone fire for medium heat (see pages 14-15).

**2.** In a medium bowl whip the cream with the sugar and orange zest until the cream has almost doubled in volume, with soft peaks. Keep cold in the refrigerator.

**3.** Halve and pit the apricots. In a small saucepan over low heat, melt the butter, and then add the sugar and almond extract and stir until the mixture is smooth, 1 to 2 minutes.

Remove the saucepan from the heat. Brush the apricot halves all over with the butter mixture.

**4.** Brush the cooking grate clean. Grill the apricot halves over ***direct medium heat***, with the lid open, until browned in spots and warm throughout, 4 to 6 minutes, turning once or twice. Swap their positions as needed for even cooking. While the apricots are grilling, lightly dust the pound cake slices on both sides with confectioners' sugar, tapping off the excess. Grill the pound cake slices over ***direct medium heat***, with the lid open, until the slices are well marked and warm, 30 to 60 seconds, turning once.

**5.** Place a slice of pound cake on each plate and arrange the apricot halves on top. Spoon some whipped cream over the apricots and sprinkle toasted almonds on top. Serve warm.

**Makes 6 servings**

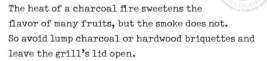

The heat of a charcoal fire sweetens the flavor of many fruits, but the smoke does not. So avoid lump charcoal or hardwood briquettes and leave the grill's lid open.

# Warm Sticky Bananas with Raspberry Sorbet

**Prep time: 10 minutes**
**Grilling time: 3 to 4 minutes**

> 4   small bananas, firm but ripe
> 2   tablespoons unsalted butter
> 1   tablespoon dark brown sugar
> 1   tablespoon fresh lime juice
> 4   large scoops raspberry sorbet
> 1   cup pistachios, coarsely chopped

**1.** Using charcoal briquettes, prepare a two-zone fire for medium heat (see pages 14-15).

**2.** Cut each banana in half lengthwise but leave the skins attached. They will help the bananas hold their shape on the grill.

**3.** Brush the cooking grate clean. In a 9 x 13-inch, heavy-duty foil pan combine the butter, sugar, and lime juice. Place the pan over ***direct medium heat***, with the lid open, to melt the butter and sugar.

**4.** When the butter and sugar are melted, slide the pan over indirect heat. Use long-handled tongs to dip the banana halves, cut sides down, in the butter mixture. Lift each banana half out of the pan, allowing the excess butter to drip back in the pan, and then place it, cut side down, over ***direct medium heat***. With the lid open, grill the banana halves until golden brown and warm, 2 to 3 minutes, without turning. Return them to the pan. If desired, keep them warm there for a few minutes.

**5.** Using insulated mitts, move the pan to a work surface. Carefully peel the banana halves without breaking them apart. Cut each banana half crosswise into 2 or 3 pieces. Scoop the sorbet into serving bowls. Arrange the banana pieces over or around the sorbet. Sprinkle the pistachios over the top.

**Makes 4 servings**

Banana skins hold the shape of the fruit on the grill and in the pan. Peel just before serving.

# Mango Ice Cream Pie with Coconut Shavings

**Prep time: 20 to 30 minutes**
**Freezer time: 2 hours**

> 1   quart vanilla ice cream
> 1   pint mango sorbet
> 1   purchased or homemade
>      8- or 9-inch graham cracker crust
> ½   cup sweetened flaked coconut
> ½   pint heavy cream
> 2   tablespoons granulated sugar
> ¼   teaspoon pure vanilla extract

**1.** Preheat the oven to 350°F.

**2.** In a medium bowl mound scoops of all the vanilla ice cream and mango sorbet. Let soften for a few minutes. Stir to combine in big swirls. Carefully spread and press the ice cream mixture into the crust, smoothing it out on top. Chill it in the freezer while you prepare the topping.

**3.** Spread the flaked coconut in a single layer on a baking sheet. Bake until lightly toasted, probably 5 to 10 minutes but start checking after 3 minutes. The coconut browns quickly.

**4.** In a medium bowl whip the cream, sugar, and vanilla until firm peaks form. Spread the whipped cream mixture on top of the ice cream. Sprinkle toasted coconut on top. Freeze until firm, about 2 hours. Serve cold.

**Makes about 12 servings**

> For great variations, use lemon, orange, or pineapple sorbet with the vanilla ice cream.

Warm Sticky Bananas with Raspberry Sorbet

Mango Ice Cream Pie with Coconut Shavings

RESOURCES

# RED MEAT

**TYPES OF RED MEAT FOR THE GRILL**

| Tender cuts for grilling | Moderately tender cuts for grilling | Bigger cuts for searing and grill-roasting | Tougher cuts for barbecuing |
|---|---|---|---|
| Beef tenderloin (filet mignon) steak | Beef top sirloin | Beef whole tenderloin | Brisket |
| Beef rib steak/rib-eye steak | Beef flank steak | Beef tri-tip roast | Beef ribs |
| Beef porterhouse steak | Beef hanger steak | Beef standing rib roast (prime rib) | Lamb shoulder |
| Beef T-bone steak | Beef skirt steak | Beef strip loin | |
| New York strip | Beef flatiron steak | Rack of veal | |
| Lamb loin chop | Veal shoulder blade chop | Rack of lamb | |
| Lamb sirloin chop | Lamb shoulder blade chop | Leg of lamb | |
| Veal loin chop | Lamb sirloin chop | | |

## How to Trim Brisket

1. The thick layer of fat on top of a brisket will protect the meat below as it cooks for 10 to 15 hours.

2. Slip a sharp knife under the membrane on the underside and remove it.

3. Also remove the hard fat near the pointed end of the brisket.

4. The brisket should look like this before you season it and barbecue it.

## Prime Cut vs. Choice Cut

The United States Department of Agriculture (USDA) grades beef based on the age of the animal and the way that fat is distributed throughout the meat. If you shop at premier meat markets or eat at fancy steakhouses, you can find Prime steaks, which usually come from young animals with abundant marbling of fat. All those milky flecks of fat add up to fantastic flavor and tenderness.

Most often you will find Choice steaks instead. Though they don't have as many flecks of fat, they do have the potential for amazing flavors and textures, that is, if you cook them right.

## When Is It Done?

Recognizing the moment when a big piece of red meat has reached the degree of doneness you want is actually quite simple. Stick the probe of an instant-read thermometer into the thickest part of the meat. When the internal temperature is 5 to 10 degrees below what you ultimately want to eat, take the meat off the grill. That's because larger pieces of meat, such as a beef strip loin or a leg of lamb, retain quite a bit of heat as they "rest" at room temperature. They continue to cook.

For optimal safety, the USDA recommends cooking red meat to 145°F (final temperature) and ground red meat to 160°F. The USDA believes that 145°F is medium rare, but virtually all chefs today believe medium rare is closer to 130°F. The chart below compares chef standards with USDA recommendations. Ultimately, it is up to you what doneness you choose.

Checking for the doneness of steaks and chops is a little more difficult with an instant-read thermometer because you need to position the sensing "dimple" of the probe right in the center of the meat. It's easy to miss the center and get an inaccurate reading, so I recommend learning to use the "touch test." Most raw steaks are as soft as the fleshiest part of your thumb when your hand is relaxed. As they cook, the steaks get firmer and firmer. If you press your first finger and thumb together and press the fleshiest part of your thumb again, the firmness is very close to that of a rare steak. If you press your middle finger and thumb together, the firmness on your thumb is very close to that of a medium rare steak.

If you are still not sure of the doneness, take the steak off the grill and put the best-looking side (presentation side) facing down on a cutting board. With the tip of a sharp knife, make a little cut in the middle so you can see the color of the meat inside. If the color is still too red, put it back on the grill. Otherwise, get the rest of the meat off the grill and pat yourself on the back. Before you serve the steaks, feel their firmness and remember that for the next time you use the touch test.

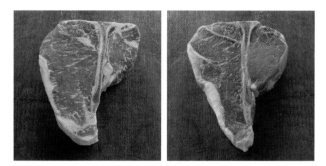

Prime beef.                    Choice beef.

Checking doneness with a thermometer.

Using the "touch test"          Nicking and peeking at
for doneness.                   the doneness.

| DONENESS | CHEF STANDARDS | USDA STANDARDS |
|----------|----------------|----------------|
| Rare | 120° to 125°F | n/a |
| Medium rare | 125° to 135°F | 145°F |
| Medium | 135° to 145°F | 160°F |
| Medium well | 145° to 155°F | n/a |
| Well done | 155°F + | 170°F |

# Brown Is Better

Whichever cut of meat you choose, and whatever its grade might be, you'll get the most flavor from it when the surface is cooked to a deep brown color. When sugars and proteins in the meat are heated by the grill, they produce literally hundreds of flavors and aromas. That's why so many recipes in this chapter involve searing over direct heat. A lot of people will tell you that searing seals in moisture, but that theory has been debunked. Instead, searing develops a layer of incredible flavor and also some nice texture.

Wet meat doesn't sear, it steams, so be sure to pat the surface dry with paper towels before grilling.

Salt can also affect searing. I recommend waiting to salt red meat until 20 to 30 minutes before grilling because, over a longer period of time, salt pulls blood and juices from inside the meat, making the surface wet. Salt does, however, need to go on before grilling. Salt added afterwards doesn't penetrate very well.

| BEEF | THICKNESS/WEIGHT | APPROXIMATE GRILLING TIME |
|---|---|---|
| Steak: New York, porterhouse, rib-eye, T-bone and tenderloin | ¾ inch thick | **4 to 6 minutes** direct high heat |
| | 1 inch thick | **5 to 8 minutes:** sear 4 to 6 minutes direct high heat, grill 1 to 2 minutes indirect high heat |
| | 1¼ inches thick | **8 to 10 minutes:** sear 6 minutes direct high heat, grill 2 to 4 minutes indirect high heat |
| | 1½ inches thick | **10 to 14 minutes:** sear 6 to 8 minutes direct high heat, grill 4 to 6 minutes indirect high heat |
| | 2 inches thick | **14 to 18 minutes:** sear 6 to 8 minutes direct high heat, grill 8 to 10 minutes indirect high heat |
| Skirt steak | ¼ to ½ inch thick | **4 to 6 minutes** direct high heat |
| Flank steak | 1½ to 2 pounds, ¾ inch thick | **8 to 10 minutes** direct high heat |
| Kabob | 1 to 1½ inch cubes | **4 to 6 minutes** direct high heat |
| Tenderloin, whole | 3½ to 4 pounds | **35 to 45 minutes:** sear 15 minutes direct medium heat, grill 20 to 30 minutes indirect medium heat |
| Ground beef patty | ¾ inch thick | **8 to 10 minutes** direct high heat |
| Rib roast (prime rib), boneless | 5 to 6 pounds | **1¼ to 1¾ hours** indirect medium heat |
| Rib roast (prime rib), with bone | 8 pounds | **2½ to 3 hours:** sear 10 minutes direct medium heat, grill 2⅓ to 3 hours indirect low heat |
| Strip loin roast, boneless | 4 to 5 pounds | **50 to 60 minutes:** sear 10 minutes direct medium heat, grill 40 to 50 minutes indirect medium heat |
| Tri-tip roast | 2 to 2½ pounds | **30 to 40 minutes:** sear 10 minutes direct medium heat, grill 20 to 30 minutes indirect medium heat |
| Veal loin chop | 1 inch thick | **5 to 8 minutes:** sear 4 to 6 minutes direct high heat, grill 1 to 2 minutes indirect high heat |

Note: All cooking times are for medium-rare doneness, except ground beef (medium).

## Lamb: The Other Red Meat

When buying lamb, look for meat that is light red (not too dark) and finely grained (not coarse). The fat should be white (not yellow). A leg of lamb opens up lots of possibilities. You could cook the whole leg on a rotisserie, with or without the bone. You could grill sirloin chops from the top end of the leg. You could sear a boneless leg of lamb, then grill-roast it over indirect heat. Or you could cut the meat into cubes and make kabobs.

## Preparing Boneless Leg of Lamb

1. Begin with the fattier side facing up. Using a sharp, thin knife, remove some of the surface fat to prevent flare-ups.

2. Turn the leg over. Cut away any large clumps of fat.

3. Slide the tip of your knife under the large areas of sinew and carefully work the knife between the sinew and meat.

4. For slightly thicker sections of the leg, make an angled cut at the thickness you want and spread the meat open like a book.

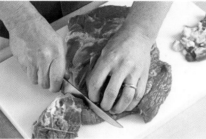

5. If one section of the leg is considerably thicker than the rest, cut it off and grill it separately.

6. In the end, you should have a leg of lamb with a relatively even thickness and 1 or 2 small sections to grill separately.

| LAMB | THICKNESS/WEIGHT | APPROXIMATE GRILLING TIME |
|---|---|---|
| Chop: loin, rib, shoulder, or sirloin | ¾ to 1½ inches thick | **8 to 12 minutes** direct medium heat |
| Leg of lamb roast, boneless, rolled | 2½ to 3 pounds | **30 to 45 minutes:** sear 10 to 15 minutes direct medium heat, grill 20 to 30 minutes indirect medium heat |
| Leg of lamb, butterflied | 3 to 3½ pounds | **30 to 45 minutes:** sear 10 to 15 minutes direct medium heat, grill 20 to 30 minutes indirect medium heat |
| Ground lamb patty | ¾ inch thick | **8 to 10 minutes** direct medium heat |
| Rack of lamb | 1 to 1½ pounds | **15 to 20 minutes:** sear 5 minutes direct medium heat, grill 10 to 15 minutes indirect medium heat |

Note: All cooking times are for medium-rare doneness, except ground lamb (medium).

# PORK

To help seasonings and smoke penetrate the meat of pork ribs, peel off the membrane clinging to the bone side.

The great pork rib dilemma: baby backs (top) or spareribs?

## What to Look for in Pork

The color and firmness of the meat are the best indicators of quality. Look for light to reddish pink meat. Avoid anything really pale or grayish. The fat should be creamy white and smooth. The texture should be firm to the touch, with a fine, smooth grain. If it is soft or watery, reject it. If the pork is packaged, it should not have much moisture in the package. Any liquid there should be clear, not cloudy.

## Peeling Pork Ribs

Spareribs and baby back ribs have a thin, tough membrane attached to the bone side. Use a blunt tool, such as a flathead screwdriver, to get under the membrane and remove it so seasonings and sauces can penetrate the meat. Slide the tool under the membrane right over one of the bones. Gradually work the tool down the bone. When the tool is about halfway down the bone, stretch the membrane up to open up a flap. It's okay if the membrane breaks at this point. Use a paper towel to get a good grip and then peel the membrane off the ribs.

## Spareribs vs. Baby Back Ribs

Butchers cut baby back ribs near the backbone of the animal, right from the area where tender chops are located. In fact, the bone from a rib chop is just one of the bones from a rack of baby back ribs. That means baby back ribs are generally a lot more tender than spareribs. Why? Spareribs are cut lower down on the side of the animal, in an area that gets more of a workout in the barnyard (or wherever). The meat is a little tougher, but it is also more flavorful.

### TYPES OF PORK FOR THE GRILL

| Tender cuts for grilling | Moderately tender cuts for grilling | Bigger cuts for searing and grill-roasting | Tougher cuts for barbecuing |
|---|---|---|---|
| Rib chop | Sirloin chop | Rack of pork | Baby back ribs |
| Loin chop | Shoulder blade steak | Sirloin loin roast | Spareribs |
| Center-cut chop | Ham steak | Center rib roast | Shoulder (Boston butt) |
| Tenderloin (whole or in medallions) | | Center loin roast | |
| | | Cured ham | |
| | | Country-style ribs | |

## When Is It Done? Think Pink!

The USDA recommends that pork is cooked to well done (170°F), but most chefs today cook it to 150°F or 160°F, when it still has some pink in the center and all the juices haven't been driven out. Of course, the doneness you choose is entirely up to you.

The pork chop on the left, with raw meat in the center, is clearly undercooked. The chop on the right, with a dry, gray appearance, is overcooked. The chop in the middle, with a little bit of pink in the center, is cooked to 150°F (just right). See how the meat gives a little under pressure.

| PORK | THICKNESS/WEIGHT | APPROXIMATE GRILLING TIME |
|---|---|---|
| Bratwurst, fresh | | **20 to 25 minutes** direct medium heat |
| Bratwurst, pre-cooked | | **10 to 12 minutes** direct medium heat |
| Pork chop, boneless or bone-in | ½ inch thick | **5 to 7 minutes** direct high heat |
| | ¾ inch thick | **6 to 8 minutes** direct high heat |
| | 1 inch thick | **8 to 10 minutes** direct medium heat |
| | 1¼ to 1½ inches thick | **10 to 12 minutes;** sear 6 minutes direct high heat, grill 4 to 6 minutes indirect high heat |
| Tenderloin | 1 pound | **15 to 20 minutes** direct medium heat |
| Loin roast, boneless | 2½ pounds | **40 to 50 minutes** direct medium heat |
| Loin roast, bone-in | 3 to 5 pounds | **1¼ to 1¾ hours** indirect medium heat |
| Pork shoulder (Boston butt), boneless | 5 to 6 pounds | **5 to 7 hours** indirect low heat |
| Pork, ground | ½ inch thick | **8 to 10 minutes** direct medium heat |
| Ribs, baby back | 1½ to 2 pounds | **3 to 4 hours** indirect low heat |
| Ribs, spareribs | 2½ to 3½ pounds | **3 to 4 hours** indirect low heat |
| Ribs, country-style, boneless | 1½ to 2 pounds | **12 to 15 minutes** direct medium heat |
| Ribs, country-style, bone-in | 3 to 4 pounds | **1½ to 2 hours** indirect medium heat |

# POULTRY

## What to Look for in Chicken

Chicken is chicken, right? Not exactly. Most supermarkets carry big national brands, or sometimes supermarkets put their own brands on these mass-produced birds raised in cages. They are low in fat, they cook quickly, and they are pretty tender, however, their flavor is pretty darn bland. Fortunately the grill provides just what they need. With a little oil, some seasonings, and maybe a sauce, they are very good on the grill.

Today we are seeing more and more premium chickens available, and usually they are worth their higher price,

though not always. Typically, these chickens are from old-fashioned breeds known more for their flavor than their plump breasts and perfectly even shape. Often called "free-range" chickens, they have access to the outdoors, or at least the freedom to wander indoors. The exercise contributes to firmer, more flavorful meat. Check them out. Any chickens you buy should have skins that fit their bodies well, not spotty or shriveled or too far overlapping. The color of the skin says little about quality, but the smell of a chicken will tell everything you need to know about freshness. If it smells funny, don't buy it.

## How to Truss a Chicken (or Game Hen)

1. With the breast side facing up, slide a 3-foot piece of twine under the back and drumsticks.

2. Cross the twine just above the drumsticks.

3. Wrap the twine around the drumsticks and pull toward the outside to bring the drumsticks together.

4. Pull the twine tightly along each side of the chicken between the joints of the drumsticks and the thighs.

5. Tie the two ends of twine together between the neck bone and the top of the breast. Pull tightly to bring the legs up against the breast.

6. After you cut off any dangling twine, the chicken is ready for grill-roasting or cooking on a rotisserie.

White breast meat is perfectly tasty at an internal temperature of 165°F, but I prefer dark leg/thigh meat cooked a little further. At 180°F, it has a richer taste and texture.

## Poultry: When Is It Done?

The USDA recommends cooking poultry until the internal temperature reaches 165°F. Keep in mind that in whole birds the internal temperature will rise 5 to 10 degrees during resting.

Check the thigh meat by inserting the probe of a thermometer in the thickest part (but not touching the bone). If you don't have a thermometer, insert a thin knife between the thigh and drumstick. The juices should run clear and the meat should no longer be pink at the bone.

| POULTRY | WEIGHT | APPROXIMATE GRILLING TIME |
| --- | --- | --- |
| Chicken breast, boneless, skinless | 6 to 8 ounces | **8 to 12 minutes** direct medium heat |
| Chicken thigh, boneless, skinless | 4 ounces | **8 to 10 minutes** direct high heat |
| Chicken breast, bone-in | 10 to 12 ounces | **30 to 40 minutes** indirect medium heat |
| Chicken pieces, bone-in leg/thigh | | **30 to 40 minutes** indirect medium heat |
| Chicken wing | 2 to 3 ounces | **18 to 20 minutes** direct medium heat |
| Chicken, whole | 3½ to 4½ pounds | **1 to 1½ hours** indirect medium heat |
| Cornish game hen | 1½ to 2 pounds | **50 to 60 minutes** indirect high heat |
| Turkey breast, boneless | 2½ pounds | **1 to 1¼ hours** indirect medium heat |
| Turkey, whole, unstuffed | 10 to 12 pounds | **2½ to 3½ hours** indirect low heat |
| | 13 to 15 pounds | **3½ to 4½ hours** indirect low heat |
| Duck breast, boneless | 10 to 12 ounces | **9 to 12 minutes:** grill 3 to 4 minutes direct low heat, grill 6 to 8 minutes indirect high heat |
| Duck, whole | 5½ to 6 pounds | **40 minutes** indirect high heat |

# FISH

The differences between farm-raised fish (left) and wild-caught fish (right) only begin with appearances. Wild fish have much deeper flavors, too.

Grill thick fish fillets with the skin side up first. Turn them only when they release cleanly from the grate.

## Choosing the Perfect Fish

The first thing to know is that firm fish and seafood are easiest to grill. The meatier they are, the better they hold together as they cook and as you turn them over. Many tender fish work nicely, too. Though they require a little more care. The chart at the bottom of this page features many of your widely available choices.

Feel free to substitute within the categories. If you find two fish with similar textures cut into similar portions, just replace one for the other.

## Five Keys to Prevent Sticking

**1. High heat.** Fish comes off the grate after a delicate crust of caramelization develops between the flesh and grate. That requires heat, usually high heat.

**2. A clean grate.** Use a brass-bristle brush to get the grate really clean.

**3. A little oil.** Coat the fish on all sides with a thin layer of oil, but don't oil the grate.

**4. A lot of patience.** Leave the fish alone. Caramelization happens faster when the fish stays in place on the hot grate. Keep the lid down as much as possible and turn the fish only once.

**5. Good timing.** The first side down on the grate will be the side that eventually faces you on the plate. Grill it a few minutes longer than the second side and it will release more easily and look fabulous on the plate, with picture-perfect grill marks.

## TYPES OF FISH FOR THE GRILL

| Firm fillets and steaks | Medium-firm fillets and steaks | Tender fillets | Whole fish | Shellfish |
|---|---|---|---|---|
| Swordfish | Monkfish | Striped bass | Red snapper | Shrimp |
| Tuna | Halibut | Bluefish | Striped bass | Scallops |
| Salmon | Mahi-mahi | Trout | Grouper | Lobster |
| Grouper | Mackerel | | Bluefish | Oysters |
| Squid | Chilean sea bass | | Mackerel | Mussels |
| | Red snapper | | Trout | Clams |

## Doneness

Overcooking fish is a crime. With almost every kind of fish, you should get it off the grill before it flakes by itself. You are looking for an  internal temperature of 125°F to 130°F, but that's tough to measure with fillets or steaks, so rely on the internal appearance (the whitish color of the fish should be opaque all the way to the center), as well as the times given in the recipes and in the chart below.

Shellfish don't flake, but they turn an opaque, pearly white color at the center when they are cooked. The only way to know for sure how the center looks is to cut into it, so plan on sacrificing one or two shellfish (a nice little snack for the chef, if they are done).

In this photo, the shrimp on the left is underdone, the right one is overdone, and the one in the middle is just right.

| FISH | THICKNESS/WEIGHT | APPROXIMATE GRILLING TIME |
|---|---|---|
| Fish, fillet or steak<br>   Includes halibut, red snapper, salmon,<br>   sea bass, swordfish, and tuna | ¼ to ½ inch thick | **3 to 5 minutes** direct high heat |
| | ½ to 1 inch thick | **5 to 10 minutes** direct high heat |
| | 1 to 1¼ inches thick | **10 to 12 minutes** direct high heat |
| Fish, whole | 1 pound | **15 to 20 minutes** indirect medium heat |
| | 2 to 2½ pounds | **20 to 30 minutes** indirect medium heat |
| | 3 pounds | **30 to 45 minutes** indirect medium heat |
| Shrimp | 1½ ounces | **2 to 4 minutes** direct high heat |
| Scallop | 1½ ounces | **4 to 6 minutes** direct high heat |
| Mussel (discard any that do not open) | | **5 to 6 minutes** direct high heat |
| Clam (discard any that do not open) | | **6 to 8 minutes** direct high heat |
| Oyster | | **2 to 4 minutes** direct high heat |
| Lobster tail | | **7 to 11 minutes** direct medium heat |

Note: General rule for grilling fish: 4 to 5 minutes per ½ inch thickness; 8 to 10 minutes per 1 inch thickness.

# VEGETABLES

Chile peppers range from fiery hot (far left) to mildly sweet (far right): habanero, Thai, cayenne, serrano, Fresno, jalapeño, poblano, and red bell.

## The Five Essentials

**1 Grill what's growing at the time.** Vegetables in season locally have big advantages over whatever has been shipped from across the world. They are riper, so they taste better. That means you can grill them simply with great results. Plus, they cost less.

**2 Expose as much surface area as possible.** Cut each vegetable to give you the biggest area to put in direct contact with the cooking grate. The more direct contact the better the flavors will be. For example, rather than cutting a zucchini crosswise into round circles, cut it lengthwise to expose more of the interior.

**3 Use the good oil.** Vegetables need oil to prevent sticking and burning. Neutral oils like canola oil will do the job fine, but an extra virgin olive oil provides the added benefit of improving the flavor of virtually every vegetable. Brush on just enough to coat each side thoroughly but not so much that the vegetables would drip oil and cause flare-ups. Season the vegetables generously with salt and pepper (some of it will fall off). For more flavors, marinate the vegetables at room temperature for 20 minutes to 1 hour in olive oil, vinegar, garlic, herbs, and spices.

**4 Baste now and then.** Vegetables have a lot of water that evaporates quickly on a hot grill. That's good news for flavor because as the water evaporates the real vegetable flavors get more intense. But some vegetables, especially mushrooms, are prone to shrinking and drying out when they lose water, so if they start to wrinkle, brush them with a little oil.

**5 Stay in the zone.** Just about everything from asparagus to zucchini tends to cook best over direct medium heat. The temperature on the grill's thermometer (if your grill has one) should be somewhere between 350°F and 450°F. If any parts get a little too dark, turn the vegetables over. Otherwise turn them as few times as possible.

## When Is It Done?

Each vegetable has its own character. The right doneness for one type may be quite different than another. And personal preference plays as big a role here as it does with red meat. I like firm vegetables such as onions and fennel to be somewhere between crisp and tender. If you want them softer, grill them a few minutes longer, although watch them carefully for burning. The grill intensifies the sweetness of vegetables quickly and that can lead to burning. Also, cut the vegetables as evenly as you can. A ½-inch thickness is right for most of them. If one edge is much thinner than the other, it tends to burn before the others are done.

| VEGETABLES | THICKNESS/SIZE | APPROXIMATE GRILLING TIME |
|---|---|---|
| Artichoke (10 to 12 ounces) | whole | **14 to 18 minutes:** boil 10 to 12 minutes; cut in half and grill 4 to 6 minutes direct medium heat |
| Asparagus | ½-inch diameter | **4 to 6 minutes** direct medium heat |
| Beet (6 ounces) | | **1 to 1½ hours** indirect medium heat |
| Bell pepper | whole | **10 to 15 minutes** direct medium heat |
| Bell/Chile pepper | ¼-inch slices | **6 to 8 minutes** direct medium heat |
| Carrot | 1-inch diameter | **7 to 11 minutes:** boil 4 to 6 minutes, grill 3 to 5 minutes direct high heat |
| Corn, husked | | **10 to 15 minutes** direct medium heat |
| Corn, in husk | | **25 to 30 minutes** direct medium heat |
| Eggplant | ½-inch slices | **8 to 10 minutes** direct medium heat |
| Fennel | ¼-inch slices | **10 to 12 minutes** direct medium heat |
| Garlic | whole | **45 to 60 minutes** indirect medium heat |
| Mushroom, shiitake or button | | **8 to 10 minutes** direct medium heat |
| Mushroom, portabello | | **10 to 15 minutes** direct medium heat |
| Onion | halved | **35 to 40 minutes** indirect medium heat |
| | ½-inch slices | **8 to 12 minutes** direct medium heat |
| Potato | whole | **45 to 60 minutes** indirect medium heat |
| | ½-inch slices | **14 to 16 minutes** direct medium heat |
| Potato, new | halved | **15 to 20 minutes** direct medium heat |
| Scallion | whole | **3 to 4 minutes** direct medium heat |
| Squash, acorn (1½ pounds) | halved | **40 to 60 minutes** indirect medium heat |
| Sweet potato | whole | **50 to 60 minutes** indirect medium heat |
| | ¼-inch slices | **8 to 10 minutes** direct medium heat |
| Tomato, garden | ½-inch slices | **2 to 4 minutes** direct medium heat |
| | halved | **6 to 8 minutes** direct medium heat |
| Tomato, plum | halved | **6 to 8 minutes** direct medium heat |
| | whole | **8 to 10 minutes** direct medium heat |
| Zucchini | ½-inch slices | **3 to 5 minutes** direct medium heat |
| | halved | **4 to 6 minutes** direct medium heat |

# { SAFETY NOTES }

## DANGER

**1.** Charcoal grills are designed for outdoor use only. If used indoors, toxic fumes will accumulate and cause serious bodily injury or death.

**2.** Do not add charcoal starter fluid or charcoal impregnated with charcoal starter fluid to hot or warm charcoal.

**3.** Do not use gasoline, alcohol, or other highly volatile fluids to ignite charcoal. If using charcoal starter fluid, remove any fluid that may have drained through the bottom vents before lighting the charcoal.

**4.** Do not leave infants, children, or pets unattended near a hot grill.

**5.** Do not use a grill within five feet of any combustible material. Combustible materials include, but are not limited to, wood or treated wood decks, patios, or porches.

**6.** Do not use a grill unless all parts are in place. Make sure the ash catcher is properly attached to the legs underneath the bowl of the grill.

## FOOD SAFETY TIPS

**1.** Wash your hands thoroughly with hot, soapy water before starting any meal preparation and after handling fresh meat, fish, and poultry.

**2.** Do not defrost meat, fish, or poultry at room temperature. Defrost in the refrigerator.

**3.** Never place cooked food on the same plate the raw food was on.

**4.** Wash all plates and cooking utensils which have come into contact with raw meats or fish with hot, soapy water and rinse.

## HELPFUL HINTS

**1.** Resist the urge to use a spatula to press down on foods such as burgers. You'll squeeze out all that wonderful flavor.

**2.** A light coating of oil will help brown your food evenly and keep it from sticking to the cooking grate. Always brush or spray oil on your food, not the cooking grate.

## WARNING

**1.** Keep the grill in a level position at all times.

**2.** Remove the lid from the grill while lighting and getting the charcoal started.

**3.** Always put charcoal on top of the charcoal grate and not directly into the bottom of the bowl.

**4.** Do not place a chimney starter on or near any combustible surfaces.

**5.** Never touch the cooking or charcoal grate or the grill to see if they are hot.

**6.** Use insulated mitts to protect hands while cooking or adjusting the vents.

**7.** Use proper barbecuing tools with long, heat-resistant handles.

**8.** Use the hook on the inside of the lid to hang the lid on the side of the bowl of the grill. Avoid placing a hot lid on carpet or grass. Do not hang the lid on the bowl handle.

**9.** To extinguish the coals, place the lid on the bowl and close all of the vents (dampers). Make sure that the vents/dampers on the lid and the bowl are completely closed. Do not use water as it will damage the porcelain finish.

**10.** To control flare-ups, place the lid on the grill and close the top vent about halfway. Do not use water.

**11.** Handle and store hot electric starters carefully. Do not place starters on or near any combustible surfaces.

**12.** Keep electrical cords away from the hot surfaces of the grill.

# INDEX

MY NOTES

MY NOTES

MY NOTES

MY NOTES

MY NOTES

MY NOTES

MY NOTES

MY NOTES